The Administration

of Interstate

Compacts

The Administration of Interstate Compacts

By *Richard H. Leach*

and *Redding S. Sugg, Jr.*

GREENWOOD PRESS, PUBLISHERS
NEW YORK

Preface

This book is the outgrowth of a project begun when the authors were on the staff of the Southern Regional Education Board, which, as an interstate compact agency, desired information about the administrative practices of other agencies in this category. There were no sources to which to turn for such information, and so the Board itself sought to compile the facts. Originally, the study was limited to the compact agencies in which the states party to the Southern Regional Education Compact participated. It was subsequently broadened, however, to include all compact agencies operative in the United States at the time the research was done. Dr. Leach began the study, and Dr. Sugg joined him when the decision was made to expand it. The collaboration indicated by joint authorship has been unusually thorough. Both authors must therefore be held responsible for every passage.

The authors are indebted to a number of persons and organizations. The Southern Regional Education Board

v

has sponsored the publication as well as the preparation of the book, and virtually the entire professional staff has made his or her contribution to the final product. Every other compact agency has been uniformly gracious about supplying data. The authors are particularly grateful to Frederick W. Zimmermann and Mitchell L. Wendell for their detailed and constructive criticism and to Brevard Crihfield and the Council of State Governments for their help and encouragement. Other debts are acknowledged in text and notes, and still others, more difficult to specify but nonetheless important to the enterprise, are regretfully omitted from mention for lack of space.

March 19, 1959   R. H. L.
                                                     R. S. S.

Contents

The Administration

of Interstate

Compacts

1: The Development of Interstate
Agencies Under the Compact Clause

In recent years, American states have established, with the actual or implied consent of Congress, some thirty interstate compact agencies. They are distinguishable from state administration and from federal agencies and so constitute an identifiable species of public administration within the federal system. They are founded upon interstate compacts which deal with subjects ranging from the allocation of waters to higher education. Known usually as commissions or boards, they own property, exercise extensive powers, employ executive staffs, and direct many important, long-term projects in the public interest. The oldest has been at work for thirty-seven years. Negotiations to create several are now in progress. Active and numerous though they are, the interstate compact agencies hardly exist in the public consciousness; and little attention has been paid them in scholarly and professional circles. The present study is

3

perhaps the first attempt to examine the operative rather than the merely legal and theoretical aspects of this development in American government.

Although compact agencies are relatively new on the scene, the use of interstate compacts is as old as the United States itself. Before the Revolution, intercolonial agreements were fairly common, and the custom was continued by the states as a matter of course under the Articles of Confederation. One of the most famous compacts in American history, the Potomac River Compact between Maryland and Virginia, was concluded in 1785.[1] The Articles, while recognizing the custom, protected the Confederation against possibly dangerous combinations of its parts by providing that ". . . no two or more states shall enter into any treaty, confederation or alliance whatever between them, without the consent of the United States in Congress assembled, verifying accurately the purposes for which the same is to be entered into, and how long it shall continue." [2] No other restrictions were imposed by the Articles, and the uses to which the states put compacts did not demonstrate the need for any.

The Potomac River Compact was a stepping-stone to the Constitutional Convention of 1787, where sentiment left the question of interstate compacts as it stood. Compacts do not seem to have been discussed except in connection with proposed limitations on the powers of the states, and the Convention carried over the Compact

[1] The Maryland legislature repealed its approval of the Compact as of June 1, 1957.
[2] Article VI.

provision of the Articles into the new Constitution virtually intact. The Committee of Detail only simplified the earlier phraseology, substituting for the Articles' "treaty, confederation or alliance" the more appropriate terms "agreement" and "compact." [3] As adopted, Article I, Section 10, of the Constitution (known familiarly as the Compact Clause), declared that ". . . no State shall, without the consent of Congress . . . enter into any agreement or compact with another State. . . ." It did not make clear how consent was to be given, much to the later confusion of Congress and the courts. The provision was obviously permissive, however, and the states had recourse to it almost at once. The first compact under the Constitution was concluded between Kentucky and Virginia in 1789.

For many years the states made very little use of compacts. Only twenty-one became effective between 1789 and 1900, and these were used only as last resorts to settle boundary and jurisdictional disputes between pairs of states. None of these early compacts created a permanent administrative agency or involved as many as three states. No one during all that time—whether governors, legislators, or constitutional lawyers and scholars—considered the compact as an instrument for the positive exercise of power. It was regarded as a means of adjustment, as an alternative to judicial settlement, as an end in itself.

[3] The term "compact" was not in general use but appeared in the plan presented to the Convention by Charles Pinckney, which may be its source; it was not used in the Articles of Confederation.

During the twentieth century, however, a revolution has occurred in the conception and so in the use of interstate compacts. Once used rarely and for the narrowest of purposes, compacts have been developed at the rate of several a year for ever broader application in recent decades. Twenty-one went into effect during the 110 years before 1900; in the 56 years following, 77 were concluded. Others are pending before Congress or state legislatures. Almost half of the latter-day compacts have established permanent interstate agencies to administer the programs they call for. The interstate compact agencies have provided a new dimension for state power. They permit the states to take continuing cooperative action in fields where they cannot act effectively or do not wish to act alone, fields which might fall by default to the federal power if not occupied through the initiative of the states.

The growing tendency to establish interstate compact agencies results in part from the fact that the problems and opportunities of state government have become vastly complex during the past fifty years. Many problems which the states must handle involve areas larger than that within the boundaries of any given state. As the nation's population has grown, particularly in urban areas, the states have become increasingly interdependent. Functions which used to concern only one state must now be performed on a multi-state or regional basis.

The recent popularity of interstate compacts is accounted for not only by their theoretical value but by the pragmatic success of the first compact agencies established in this century. The most important single event

in the rise of the interstate compact agency was probably
the establishment and success of the Port of New York
Authority, based on a compact concluded in 1921. Designed to attack the enormously complex problem of
developing and operating the Port of New York, the
Authority also had to function in spite of the jealousies
of the party states, New York and New Jersey. For eighty
years they had fought over the use of the facilities of the
Port and the adjacent area.[4] Every other expedient had
been exhausted when the creation by compact of a
permanent interstate agency was suggested.

The Port of New York Authority proved to be so effective in operation that its example encouraged the use of
compacts in solving two other troublesome problems of
the multi-state metropolitan area. The Interstate Sanitation Commission was created by compact in 1935 to deal
with pollution of the waters touching Connecticut, New
York, and New Jersey. In 1937, New York and New
Jersey again approached a problem—that of recreation
for the heavily concentrated population at their boundary
—by means of a compact, which created the Palisades
Interstate Park Commission to replace the existing arrangements. These two agencies were as successful as
the earlier ones, and the effect of their example was considerable throughout the nation. The widespread adoption a few years later of the Parole and Probation Compact had a still greater influence. Meanwhile, the example of a group of Western states in applying the interstate compact to the apportionment of the waters of the

[4] See Erwin W. Bard, *The Port of New York Authority* (New
York, 1942), 5–26, for a detailed account.

Colorado River by means of the Colorado River Compact of 1923 was added to the examples in the East; and thus the variety of applications to which compacts might be put began to be apparent.

Compacts and the principle of interstate administration were advocated by several groups and individuals during the 1920's and 1930's. Influenced by the effectiveness of the Port of New York Authority, the National Conference of Commissioners on Uniform State Laws appointed a Committee on Inter-State Compacts headed by Dean John H. Wigmore of Northwestern University. After careful study, this committee concluded that interstate compacts were generally applicable to many of the problems resulting from "disharmony of action or inaction" caused by the independently drafted laws of the several states. The Wigmore committee recommended further use of compacts by the states.

In 1925 the most influential single argument for the use of interstate compacts appeared. Analyzing the Compact Clause and its implications, Felix Frankfurter and James M. Landis vigorously expounded the potential values of compacts and interstate agencies. They declared that ". . . the combined legislative powers of Congress and the several States [that is, as combined in compacts] permit a wide range of permutations and combinations for governmental action. Until very recently these potentialities have been left largely unexplored. . . . Creativeness is called for to devise a great variety of legal alternatives to cope with the diverse forms of interstate interests." They also pointed out, "Conservation of natural resources is . . . making a major demand on

American statesmanship. An exploration of the possibilities of the compact idea furnishes a partial answer to one of the most intricate and comprehensive of all American problems." And, they insisted, "The imaginative adaptation of the compact idea should add considerably to reserves available to statesmen in the solution of problems presented by the growing interdependence, social and economic, of groups of States forming distinct regions." [5]

These exhortations were enthusiastically received. Christian A. Herter, for example, recently recalled the impact on him of the Frankfurter-Landis article. "At the time Justice Frankfurter's article was published," he wrote, "I was serving in the Massachusetts legislature in the lower branch. Together with a friend in the upper branch, I began to look around with the idea that there was something the States really ought to examine. . . ." [6] Herter and his colleague were not alone in their response. Almost every proposal of a new compact during the next ten years acknowledged a debt to Frankfurter and Landis, and nothing has been written since on the subject which has not credited them with helping to bring compacts out of obscurity.

Within a few years after the article by Frankfurter and Landis appeared, many influential groups endorsed the expansive use of compacts which they advocated. These

[5] Felix Frankfurter and James M. Landis, "The Compact Clause of the Constitution—A Study in Interstate Adjustments," *Yale Law Journal*, XXIV (May, 1925), 688, 699, 729.

[6] Christian A. Herter, "New Horizons for States," *National Municipal Review*, XL (April, 1957), 174.

groups included Congress,[7] the United States Chamber of Commerce, the National Resources Committee, and the National Governors' Conference.[8] Meanwhile, a considerable literature advocating the establishment of interstate compact agencies appeared. Law reviews published studies on "Industrial and Labor Adjustments by Interstate Compacts" and "Interstate Compacts for Crime Control;"[9] popular magazines featured articles with such titles as "Little Americas: Innovation in Government by Interstate Compacts";[10] and a great many pamphlets were prepared and distributed.[11] As the Supreme Court repeatedly declared unconstitutional a variety of New Deal measures to cope with depression,

[7] As early as 1911, Congress advocated use of the interstate compact to secure continuing interstate cooperation by passing the Weeks Act, which gave consent in advance to "each of the states to enter into any agreement or compact with any other state or states for the purpose of conserving the forests and water supply of those states." 36 Stat. 691 (1911).

[8] The 43rd Annual Governors' Conference went so far as to resolve that Congress should enact *general* consent-in-advance legislation, permitting the states to negotiate compacts in unspecified "broad fields of action" for which the states have primary responsibility. See *State Government*, XXIV (November, 1951), 286.

[9] The titles of articles by F. C. Wilson in *Marquette Law Review*, XX (December, 1935), 11–26; and by Gordon Dean in *American Bar Association Journal*, XXI (February, 1935), 89–91.

[10] The title of an article by Jane Perry Clark in *Survey Graphic*, XXV (January, 1936), 36–38.

[11] For example, Marshall Dimock and George C. S. Benson, *Can Interstate Compacts Succeed?* "A Public Affairs Pamphlet of the University of Chicago" (Chicago, 1937).

compacts were recommended as substitutes for federal action. Soon found wanting in this regard, the compact device nevertheless profited by the enthusiasm and interest which had been engendered. By the mid-thirties, compacts were properly understood as an expedient of state government which promised much in many fields.

The establishment of the Council of State Governments—formerly the American Legislators' Association —in 1935 brought the interstate compact a diligent and enduring ally. It is probably fair to say that the Council has followed the lead of its Eastern Regional Office and the New York Joint Legislative Committee on Interstate Cooperation in fostering the use of compacts. The eastern office and the Committee have been closely associated since the establishment of the Council, and the Committee's research staff has helped draft a number of compacts in which New York does not participate. Although the Council has had no part in the development of many compacts, it is taking an increasing interest in initiating them in various parts of the country.

One of the Council's functions is to assist the states in drafting compacts, in conducting the related research, and in establishing interstate agencies. It suggests possible uses for compacts and conducts conferences of state officials concerned with problems which might be handled by compact. Frequently the Council prepares preliminary drafts of compacts for consideration at such meetings, undertakes revisions, and follows through by arguing in support of Congressional consent. At the same time, Commissions on Interstate Cooperation or the equivalent, which are the Council's contact points in each state, stand ready to help in the adoption of compacts. Once compacts become effective and interstate agencies begin to function, the Council of State Governments sometimes assists with operational difficulties.

The several compacts concerned with the control of forest fires, for example, witness to the Council's effectiveness as promoter. The 11th General Assembly of the States, convened by the Council in 1952, praised the New England and Middle Atlantic states for leading the way in formulating such compacts and suggested "that states in other areas of the country study carefully the compact mechanism for interstate fire protection." [12] Shortly thereafter, upon indication of interest by several Southern states, the Council called a series of meetings of state forestry officials to discuss the earlier compacts in the field and to assist them in drawing up their own. The result was the conclusion in short order of the Southeastern Interstate Forest Fire Protection Compact and the South Central Interstate Forest Fire Protection Compact.

Not only do the Council and the Commissions on Interstate Cooperation sponsor compacts in these effective ways, but the ever increasing number of interstate agencies in operation provide a growing pool of knowledge and experience from which all may draw with profit. Interstate compact agencies are now so common that the processes they utilize are more and more widely understood. Thanks to the decision of the Supreme Court in the case of *West Virginia ex rel. Dyer et al., v.*

[12] *State Government,* XXVI (January, 1953), 33.

Sims, State Auditor,[13] which tested West Virginia's membership in the Ohio River Valley Water Sanitation Compact, states may also proceed in the assurance that they are on firm ground.

The Court held that a state may properly delegate "the power to make rules and decide particular cases" to an agency established by interstate compact as well as to a regular state agency.[14] Such a delegation amounts to no more than a "conventional grant of legislative power."[15] A state may not, the Court continued, withdraw from a compact delegating power to an interstate agency on the grounds that the delegation was, after all, contrary to her constitution, for she has entered into a contractual obligation not lightly to be broken. As Justice Jackson noted in his concurring opinion, "West Virginia, for internal affairs, is free to interpret her own Constitution as she will. But if the Compact system is to have vitality and integrity, she may not (retroactively) raise an issue of *ultra vires,* decide it, and release herself from an interstate obligation."[16] If a state attempts so to withdraw from an otherwise valid compact, the Supreme Court may be asked to stop her; for the "interpretation of the meaning of [a] compact [by the court] controls over a state's application of its own law through the Supremacy clause. . . ."[17]

As a result of *Dyer v. Sims,* compact agencies may operate as arms of state governments under a collective delegation of legislative power from each state involved, and the Supreme Court may be expected to sustain the

[13] 341 U.S. 22 (1950).   [14] *Ibid.,* at 30.   [15] *Ibid.,* at 31.
[16] *Ibid.,* at 35.   [17] *Ibid.,* at 33, Justice Reed, concurring.

compacts behind them whenever they are attacked on technical or legislative grounds. "Thus," comments one student of the case, "the effect of the ruling is to broaden the potentialities of interstate compacts for the establishment, and may be the impetus for a more frequent resort to, and broader application of, the interstate compact." [18]

As interstate action authorized by compact has gained assurance, the conception of the interstate compact as a form has been clarified and the *ad hoc* approach to the drafting of these instruments has given way to the sophisticated adaptation of the form to particular situations. As recently as 1934 a writer could observe that "what constitutes a compact or an agreement under the terms of the Constitution has never been comprehensively defined." [19] Since then, particularly through the work of the New York Joint Legislative Committee on Interstate Cooperation and the experience of compact agencies, the question has been considerably clarified. In the absence of Constitutional definition, the consensus is that an interstate compact is a contract; but because of the quasi-sovereign nature of the parties to an interstate compact, this is regarded as a more formal and weighty commitment than a contract involving private persons.[20] Thus the interstate compact has been recognized as "an identifiable and separate document." [21]

[18] H. B. Rubenstein, "The Interstate Compact—A Survey," *Temple Law Quarterly*, XXVII (Winter, 1954), 328.

[19] Henry Parkman, Jr., "A Single Standard," *State Government*, VII (July, 1934), 143.

[20] Cf. *Virginia v. Tennessee*, 148 U.S. 503 (1893).

[21] Frederick L. Zimmermann and Mitchell Wendell, *The Interstate Compact Since 1925* (Chicago, 1951), 42.

The Development of Interstate Agencies

The several compacts, however, vary in content and emphasis according to the circumstances under which they have been developed and applied. The compacts which create interstate agencies tend to be the most elaborate, containing such elements as the following:

1. A statement of the motives which prompt the signatory states.
2. A definition of the purposes which the compact is to realize.
3. A description of the geographical area affected.
4. A provision for an interstate agency to administer the program called for.
5. A provision for financing the program.
6. Provisions for ratifying, amending, enforcing, or terminating the compact.

A tendency toward uniformity of content and phrasing may be observed in recent compacts as the older ones are increasingly studied and the influence of such organizations as the Council of State Governments and state commissions on interstate cooperation, notably New York's, is more widely felt.

Although created by the states, compacts are indebted also to Congress for their existence since they are, according to the Constitution, the products of the combined legislative powers of Congress and the party state legislatures. Congress plays a merely formal role with regard to most compacts, however, simply granting its consent to compacts already drawn and agreed to by the party states. As a matter of fact, some compacts have gone into effect without benefit of consent legislation passed by Congress. Most particularly, it is concerned with compacts which deal with interstate waters and thus gives its most careful attention to the compacts devoted to water apportionment, the control of stream pollution, and the development and conservation of fisheries. Federal representatives often participate in the formulation and administration of such compacts in order to guarantee adequate consideration of legitimate federal interests. The Director of the U.S. Bureau of the Budget, in a memorandum to President Truman in 1952, described the steps he considered necessary to accomplish this during the drafting and negotiation of compacts.

The budget director's advice, which was used to guide the federal negotiator of the Sabine River Compact, remains one of the most effective statements of the federal attitude:

Several steps can be taken to insure this consideration [of federal interests]. First, a general preliminary report may be made to the President by the negotiator at a reasonable time prior to the date or dates on which the draft of the compact is to be submitted to the States for ratification. This report should, of course, be concerned only with matters of Federal interest and should not deal with matters purely of interest to the States. It should include a copy of the draft compact, information on the date or dates on which it will be submitted to the States, and report on the provisions included in the compact for federal participation in its administration, if the States so provide, and for the protection of the interests of the people of the United States. We believe that such a preliminary reporting procedure would be most helpful in assuring that interstate compacts reflect as clearly as possible a recognition of the respective responsibilities and prerogatives of the United States and the affected States. Second, liaison between the Federal negotiator and the interested Federal agencies during the compact negotiations can be improved and widened. The Departments of Agriculture, the Army, the Interior, Justice and Commerce and the Federal Power Commission and Federal Security Agency frequently have an interest in compacts relating to the apportionment of waters among the States. Therefore, it would seem desirable for the Federal negotiator to inform the heads of these Federal departments and agencies of the pending negotiations, prior to their commencement. Federal agencies should cooperate with the Federal negotiator in promptly making available to him any views that they may have. During the negotiations the Federal representative should keep the President advised of all important issues affecting Federal interests or administration that arise and should notify him as to the probable interest in these issues of the several Federal agencies.

Such steps to protect Federal interests, of course, should not interfere in any way with the orderly process of negotiations by the States nor limit in any respect the right of the States to submit to the Congress any proposals which the States agree upon. . . .[22]

[22] *Documents on the Use and Control of the Waters of Interstate and International Streams—Compacts, Treaties, and Adjudications* (Washington, D.C., 1956), 247–248.

The range of subject matter of the compacts which create interstate agencies is extremely impressive, as the titles of the several already mentioned will have suggested. Allocation and conservation of waters; flood control; water pollution control; management of fisheries; control of forest fires; harbor management; development of multi-state metropolitan areas; construction and operation of interstate bridges; development of interstate parks; regulation of the New York waterfront; conservation of oil; regional development of higher education; modernization of parole and probation procedures —in all of these activities the states have resorted to the compact as a device to achieve purposes which they cannot achieve severally or which, at any rate, they feel may be more effectively achieved in concert.

It may be helpful to categorize the compacts according to the sort of power and responsibility which they delegate to interstate agencies. The classification below is made in terms of the primary emphasis of the compacts, many of which naturally share characteristics with others differently classified. The first group may be thought of as *technical* and consists of the water allocation compacts. Second are the *study and recommendatory* compacts designed primarily to investigate issues, make recommendations to the constituent states, and perhaps to publicize their findings in order to persuade the proper officials to act. The third group may be distinguished as *operating,* since the compacts concerned empower the agencies they create to own and operate various facilities or institutions. From the point of view of public administration, the technical compacts are less significant than the advisory group or the operating group because more limited in the exercise of discretion. Although the least powerful in theory, the advisory compacts are often extremely influential and tend to be broader in scope than the operating ones.

The present study deals with thirty interstate agencies created by compact. They are listed below according to the distinctions just given, on the understanding that these are by no means hard and fast:

Technical

Arkansas River Compact Administration
Canadian River Commission
Pecos River Commission
Rio Grande Compact Commission
Sabine River Compact Administration
Upper Colorado River Commission
Yellowstone River Compact Commission

Study and Recommendatory

Atlantic States Marine Fisheries Commission
Bi-State Development Agency
Connecticut River Valley Flood Control Commission
Interstate Commission on the Potomac River Basin
Interstate Oil Compact Commission
Interstate Sanitation Commission
New England Board of Higher Education
New England Interstate Water Pollution Control Commission

Northeastern Interstate Forest Fire Protection Commission

Gulf States Marine Fisheries Commission

Ohio River Valley Water Sanitation Commission

Pacific Marine Fisheries Commission

Southern Regional Education Board

Western Interstate Commission on Higher Education

Operating

Breaks Interstate Park Commission

Delaware River Joint Toll Bridge Commission

Delaware River Port Authority

Lake Champlain Bridge Commission

Maine-New Hampshire Interstate Bridge Authority

Palisades Interstate Park Commission

Port of New York Authority

Tennessee-Missouri Bridge Commission

Waterfront Commission of New York Harbor

Some fifteen other interstate compacts which do not create administrative agencies will not be mentioned in this volume, because the present inquiry is concerned with agencies established by compact, rather than with compacts as such. Several compacts call for interstate agencies which have not been appointed or which, having been appointed, have not acted; these can be only glanced at although they may be very interesting. One omission should be particularly explained: the Interstate Commission on the Delaware River Basin will not be discussed because, although an interstate operation, it is not

based on a compact. Furthermore, its kind of function is represented by other organizations which will be included. Finally, at least four interstate compacts which are still being negotiated or which have not been ratified will be excluded even though they propose interstate agencies.

2: Interstate Compact Agencies: Relations
with State and Federal Governments

Agencies established by interstate compact are identified administratively with the party states rather than with the federal government. They may develop close relations with federal departments and include among their members federal officials, but they are no more a part of the federal administrative organization than any ordinary department of a state government. The use of compacts is still too new, however, for any well defined concept of the proper relations between a state and a compact agency to which it subscribes to have developed. Not only do the several legislatures which stand *in loco parentis* to a given compact agency differ in their approaches to it, but the same legislature frequently takes different attitudes toward the several compact agencies to which it is a party. Thus there may or may not be any formal relations between a legislature and an interstate compact agency. Where clearly formulated relations do exist, they are often the result of effort on the part of the compact agency.

The existence of the Commissions on Interstate Cooperation or the equivalent and of the Council of State Governments, which in some sense coordinates or at least advises the Commissions, has led many observers to speculate on the possibility of developing uniform policies toward interstate agencies. The Commission on Interstate Cooperation in each state might, the argument goes, serve as the channel of communication between the state and all of the interstate agencies in which it participates. It might direct the negotiation of compacts, guide the members of interstate compact agencies, receive and properly handle communications from these agencies, and send representatives to the Assembly of the States which the Council sponsors. Historically, it need hardly be repeated, the Council has been effective in drawing states together to formulate compacts but has had little influence on the relations between states and compact agencies at work. The Commissions on Interstate Cooperation, furthermore, have assumed few if any of the functions mentioned.

Only a few states have made a beginning in formally relating interstate compact agencies to their administrative organizations. In Missouri, for example, the Bi-State Development Agency and the Tennessee-Missouri River Bridge Commission have been brought under the state Department of Business and Administration. Minnesota placed her participation in the now inactive Tri-States Waters Commission under the supervision of the Department of Conservation. Most states, however, have ignored the problem or relied upon the essentially personal liaison which may be achieved by appointing appropriate state administrators to membership on compact commissions or boards. Unrelated to the activities of ordinary state departments and agencies, the compact agencies are left to their own devices, frequently overlooked, and sometimes forgotten altogether. In such circumstances, they have usually had to make themselves known and to develop for themselves whatever relations with the executive branches of the party governments seemed necessary or practical.

One of the more successful agencies in this regard, the Southern Regional Education Board has developed a complex system of relations, not only with various arms of the constituent state governments, but with state and private educational institutions, federal agencies, foundations, and other organizations. Although created at the suggestion of the governors of the Southern states, the Board's relation to intra-state agencies concerned with higher education was not defined in the Southern Regional Education Compact. As a result, the Board was at first very much the outsider, but gradually, through such devices as its annual Legislative Work Conference, it has made a place for itself.

The Port of New York Authority has also been successful in developing satisfactory relations with governmental units in its party states. Although it has not been formally incorporated into the administrative structure of either New York or New Jersey, it has been treated from the beginning with considerable respect by the states and has received earnest cooperation from the regular agencies of both. New York and New Jersey have adopted the same attitude toward the more recent Waterfront Commission of New York Harbor. Although such recognition does not remove either of these compact agencies from the isolation in which all such agencies operate, it does at least make informal relations easier and reduces the problem which many compact agencies face in merely asserting their existence.

As a result of their uncertain relations to parent legislatures and their exclusion from the administrative structure of their constituent states, the compact agencies operate with considerable freedom. The states have not enforced strict controls even upon the agencies which perform functions which would otherwise be carried out by intra-state agencies. The interstate compacts abound with provisions designed to limit the agencies they create, but the activities of these agencies are, in practice, little checked or supervised. Perhaps because they make small demands on state treasuries and confine their activities in most cases to specialized and technical fields, the inter-state compact agencies have been accorded greater independence than the typical intra-state agency. Only when the activities of a compact agency directly affect those of some department of a state government—or threaten to do so—does a legislator or state executive official exhibit much concern.

Although the states allow, largely through neglect, such latitude to the compact agencies, the formal, legal relations between the states and these agencies are chiefly negative. Virtually every compact is replete with devices to permit the states to investigate, supervise, consent to, limit, and even prohibit the activities of the agency it creates. Few compacts provide for any positive relations between the states and the interstate agencies. Furthermore, the statutes by which the states ratify compacts often make possible controls not provided in the compacts themselves.

The jealousy of the states appears to be unwarranted, for they have the upper hand when it counts most, during the processes of negotiation and ratification. Subscription to any interstate compact is entirely voluntary, and each state may decide freely whether or not to grant powers to interstate agencies as called for in compacts presented for legislative action. On the whole, the powers delegated to interstate compact agencies are carefully enumerated; and, although most compacts contain a "necessary and proper" clause, it has not been construed to mean an increase in the power available to the agencies established. No theory of implied powers has been developed in connection with compacts.

Moreover, the states generally withhold the most important power of all: only a few compact agencies have been granted the power to make and enforce penalties for the violation of their rulings. The vital power of enforcement remains with the states, and the compacts usually declare that the findings of the agencies they create are not binding in court. "The findings of the Commission," runs the Rio Grande River Compact, "shall not be conclusive in any court or tribunal which may be called upon to interpret or enforce this Compact." [1] Such provisions, which exist in most cases,

[1] Article XII. Compacts creating regulatory agencies are not

guarantee the states and not the interstate compact agencies the last word. Finally, whether or not a compact specifies, as the Delaware River Port Authority Compact does, that the agency may exercise only those powers "not inconsistent with the constitutions of the . . . states or of the United States"[2] or with the laws of either, all interstate compacts are so limited. No compact agency may act *ultra vires* or in an unconstitutional fashion any more successfully than intra-state agencies. The state courts are as capable of reining them in as they are of restraining any state officer or agency.

All the controls mentioned above, being fundamental to the adoption of any compact, are implicit even if not explicit in every compact, so that no particular need exists for the states to impose controls upon the agencies created by compacts. Special provisions to control compact agencies may seem redundant but may be made to guard against litigation which might arise, for example, from different provisions of several state constitutions. All compacts become part of the law of each party state upon ratification, and all compact agencies thus automatically become agencies of the several party states. A state may not acknowledge the presence of a compact agency or make room for it in its administrative structure, but the agency's position in law is nevertheless as secure as that of the oldest intra-state department. All

---

very numerous; if they increase, so will powers of enforcement of an interstate character. A "finding," as here used, is an administrative step in a regulatory adjudication or enforcement proceeding.

[2] Article IV, n.

devices for control, supervision, and direction which may be brought to bear on intra-state agencies may also be brought to bear on compact agencies. Just as ordinary state agencies require legislative support for their activities and must win legislative approval year by year, so must all but three or four compact agencies secure appropriations from their several legislatures to enable them to hire staff and carry out their mandates. The same investigations which may precede appropriations to other state agencies may be made of compact agencies, and the same restrictions placed on the use of appropriated funds. Similarly, the standing subject-matter committees of the legislatures are as competent to look into the operations of compact agencies as into those of other state agencies in the same fields. In extraordinary situations, a special legislative inquiry could be made into interstate as well as into intra-state agencies.

Nor are interstate compact agencies exempt from normal gubernatorial supervision or control. As with most state appointive officers, a governor's control over the members of a compact agency begins with their appointment. From then on, they fall under the governor's general supervisory power. In most state constitutions, the governor is empowered to require information in writing from the heads of executive departments in regard to any matter within their jurisdiction. There is no reason to assume that interstate officials are exempt from this requirement, for in relation to the compact agency they are executive heads. Certainly any reluctance on the part of a compact agency to cooperate with one of its constituent states or any unwarranted arrogation of power would come to the governor's attention as quickly as similar actions on the part of ordinary state personnel. The governor, finally, is as free to investigate such complaints about an interstate as about a regular state agency; as Brooke Graves suggests, "the possibilities of the use of the investigatory power of the governor as an instrument of coercion" or control are very great.[3]

The interstate compact agencies are also, of course, subject to judicial controls. The powers of both state and federal courts may be applied to them. They are thus peculiarly vulnerable to judicial correction in the event they overstep their prescribed roles.

In spite of this variety of proper and adequate controls, the states are still distrustful of the interstate compact agencies which they create. The reason is, probably, that, not having been integrated into state administrative systems, the compact agencies are subject to the suspicions which follow aliens. These circumstances must be taken into account in the drafting of interstate compacts, and the result has been the insertion in most compacts of elaborate controls specifically applicable to the interstate agencies.

For example, although most of the states require annual reporting by all of their agencies, virtually every interstate compact requires that the agency it creates make a special annual report to each of the participating legislatures, and in some instances to the governors as well,

[3] W. Brooke Graves, *American State Government* (New York, 1953), 381.

29

"setting forth in detail the operations and transactions conducted by it, pursuant to [the] compact. . . ." [4] There is little evidence, however, that the reports of compact agencies have been taken seriously by the legislatures that have required them. In general, they are routinely handled and often filed without being circulated to the legislators. In some cases, compact agencies submit only one copy of the annual report, a practice which makes any use of it unlikely. Questionnaires returned to the authors of this study indicate that a majority of members of legislatures party to compacts do not read the annual reports and that many do not know they are available. Whereas every governor is probably at least aware that interstate compact agencies make reports, it is doubtful that the governors make much more use of them than the legislators.

Another special control included in most compacts is the requirement that the books of the agencies they establish be available for inspection or auditing by authorized representatives of the party states or by an independent auditing firm. [5] No compact specifies what

[4] Article IV, New England Higher Education Compact. The Gulf States and the Atlantic States Marine Fisheries Compacts, the Southern Regional Education Compact, and the Interstate Compact to Conserve Oil and Gas do not require reporting, but the agencies they established have customarily done so. Some compacts are even more explicit than the New England Higher Education Compact, requiring, for instance, reports on lands acquired, receipts, and expenditures during the report year.

[5] A few compacts make independent auditing mandatory, e.g., Article VIII, Upper Colorado River Basin Compact, which declares that "all receipts and disbursement of funds handled by

action may be taken as a result, but there is no need—
no more need, indeed, than for the requirement itself.
For no state agency is immune from authorized scrutiny
of its financial operations or from prosecution if mis-
management or peculation is discovered. Some compacts
prohibit the agencies which they create from incurring
any obligations for operating expenses prior to appropriation of state funds to meet them and from pledging the
credit of any of the signatory states without specific approval of the legislature. Such prohibitions, again, only
make explicit for compact agencies what is always at
least implicit for any state agency.

Several compacts set limits beyond which the party
states may not assume responsibility for the operations
of the agencies concerned. The Connecticut River Valley Flood Control Compact, for instance, provides that
the party states will appropriate funds

*for compensation of agents and employees of the com-
mission and for office, administrative, travel and other
expenses on recommendation of the commission, subject
to limitations as follows: The Commonwealth of Massachusetts obligates itself to not more than seventy-five
hundred (7,500) dollars in any one year, the State of
New Hampshire . . . to not more than one thousand
(1,000) dollars . . . , the State of Vermont . . . to not
more than one thousand (1,000) dollars . . . , and the*

---

the Commission shall be audited yearly by a qualified independent public accountant and the report of the audit shall be
included in and become a part of the annual report of the
Commission."

31

State of Connecticut . . . to not more than sixty-five hundred (6,500) dollars. . . .[6]

The Potomac River Basin Compact provides that the total of the sums contributed by all the signatory bodies shall not exceed $30,000 per annum.[7] In fact no legislature guarantees any state agency an unlimited appropriation. The difference between intra-state and compact agencies, however, is that any limitation on appropriations for a purely state agency may be waived by a simple legislative act, whereas to alter a limitation on appropriations specified in a compact for an interstate agency might require an amendment of the compact, a long and complicated procedure.

Such a financial ceiling as that imposed by the Potomac River Basin Compact would seem to confine the activities of the agency it creates to whatever operations or services may be obtained for this sum and thus possibly to inhibit attainment of the objectives of the Compact. Recently, as a matter of fact, the Interstate Commission for the Potomac River Basin declared that because of the limited contributions of its constituents, "There are areas of interest, and activities, now open to the Commission, which remain largely untouched. The work of the Commission could be greatly expanded if it were not for limitation of funds."[8] Accordingly, the Commission has proposed removing the ceiling.

Probably no other form of control over interstate

[6] Article VII.   [7] Article III.
[8] Interstate Commission for the Potomac River Basin, *News Letter,* XIII (September, 1957).

agencies is so effective as limitations on appropriations, at least where appropriations are the sole source of support. Few compacts impose specific limitations,[9] however, and many interstate compact agencies are only partially dependent on appropriations. The two port authorities, the three bridge commissions, and the two park commissions are self-supporting. One or two of these received state aid to begin with but once in operation were required to support themselves on fees, tolls, and other charges, or on bonds issued in anticipation of revenue. Many of the recommendatory agencies receive income not only from appropriations but from executive agencies of the party states, from the federal government, and from private foundations. Most of the income from such sources must be used for program activities and not for operating expenses, but it frees the agency from dependence on the legislatures in developing program. Finally, the work of the water allocation commissions is underwritten in part by the U.S. Geological Survey. In practice, then, the interstate compact agencies are less controlled than might be supposed by their constituent states' power of the purse.

Most of the compacts make the party states responsible in some degree for financing the interstate agencies. At one extreme, the New England Higher Education Compact seems to bind the states to support the New England Board of Higher Education in advance by declaring that each state "agrees that it will from time to

[9] The Interstate Sanitation Compact and the New England Interstate Water Pollution Control Compact also establish ceilings on financial contributions by party states.

time make available to the Board such funds as may be required for the expenses of the Board as authorized under the terms of this compact." [10] More common are provisions like that of the Gulf States Marine Fisheries Compact, which merely declares that the "operating expenses of the . . . Commission shall be borne by the states party thereto." [11] At the other extreme, two compacts relieve the states of financial responsibility altogether. Article VII of the Interstate Oil Compact denies the responsibility of the party states to support the Interstate Oil Compact Commission, and the Bi-State Development Compact ignores the matter entirely. Yet, although the Bi-State Development Agency has hardly been able to begin operations for lack of money, the Interstate Oil Compact Commission, voluntarily supported by the states, has flourished. Viewed as controls rather than as enabling devices, the financial provisions of interstate compacts appear to be largely redundant, for there is no way to force a legislature to make a particular appropriation in any case; and in practice at least one interstate compact agency has developed in the face of the refusal of the states to bind themselves to any financial support at all.

A third type of control sometimes expressed in compacts is the power of the governors of the party states to remove members of interstate bodies upon charges and after a hearing. "Each member of the commission," declares the Palisades Interstate Park Compact, "may be removed from office for neglect of duty or misconduct in office by the governor of the state of which such member

[10] Article VI.   [11] Article XII.

is a citizen after giving such member a copy of the charges and an opportunity of being publicly heard or by counsel or both in his own defense, upon not less than ten days' notice." [12] The Port of New York Authority Compact and one or two others include similar provisions. They seem to be unnecessary language, however, since the members of interstate commissions are also state officials and may be removed by the same processes. Actually, no member of any interstate body has ever been removed under such provisions.

Perhaps in recognition of the fact that the danger in compact administration lies not so much in officials who abuse their powers as in those who do not use them at all, a few recent compacts contain clauses which permit the governors to remind members of interstate agencies of their duty. The Atlantic States Marine Fisheries Compact, for example, provides that the continued absence of representation or of any particular representative from commission meetings shall be brought to the attention of the appropriate governor.[13] The Palisades Interstate Park Compact, the Breaks Interstate Park Compact, and the Lake Champlain Bridge Compact require an oath of commissioners that they will perform the duties of their offices to the best of their ability. Since it is common practice to require certain state officials to take such oaths, the extension of the requirement to interstate officials does not in fact subject them to special treatment although it may be so intended.

[12] Article II.
[13] Article X. The Pacific Marine Fisheries Compact contains the same language.

If the purpose of such oaths is to assure proper conduct in office, and if a special device to guarantee it is thought necessary, the Port of New York Authority Compact, the Maine-New Hampshire Interstate Bridge Compact, and the Tennessee-Missouri Bridge Compact contain a different sort of provision which is probably more effective. "Each state reserves the right hereafter," reads the Maine-New Hampshire Compact, "to provide by law for the exercise of a veto power by the governor thereof over any action of any commissioner appointed therefrom." [14] The veto power, which has rarely been used, is available also to disapprove stands on policy as well as conduct. That would seem to be a more cogent reason for including such a provision, for it might seem that an interstate agency could make policy decisions counter to the interests of party states which would be helpless, at least for a time, to prevent the agency from acting accordingly. The fact that so few compacts include veto provisions may be explained by the custom among interstate officials of clearing in advance with their governors or other figures in the executive or legislative branches of their home states all major policy decisions.

Indeed, the Port of New York Authority was required by its Compact to submit its original plans to the legislatures of both party states before it acted under them, and it must still get specific legislative approval of supplemental plans. The Delaware River Port Authority Compact takes the same means of rendering major policy decisions impossible without legislative approval. Pro-

[14] Article X.

visions of this sort largely obviate the need for a veto. Even in the absence of such requirements—they do not appear in most compacts—members of interstate bodies are usually careful to act in general accordance with state policy. To do otherwise would be to make the agency's operations difficult if not impossible, for interstate agencies, like any other units of government, operate within the realm of practical politics.

Further controls in the form of a variety of procedural requirements which interstate agencies must meet are also common in compacts. The large proportion of the texts of compacts devoted to such requirements indicates the importance the states attach to them as means of control. With almost no exceptions, compacts specify either that a majority of the members of the agencies they establish shall constitute a quorum for the transaction of business or that a quorum shall consist of a specified number of members from each state. The purpose and effect of such requirements, of course, is to protect the party states against action at a meeting from which their representatives are absent. The states are no doubt justified in imposing this type of control, and most compacts provide further that no action of the interstate agency shall be binding unless a majority of the members shall have been present and shall have voted aye. Some compacts go so far as to give each state one vote, regardless of the number of representatives, and to require that "every decision, authorization or other action shall require a unanimous vote." [15]

Of all the compacts, the Interstate Oil Compact pro-

[15] Arkansas River Compact, Article VIII, D.

vides the most intricate method of voting to protect the party states. It has never been used, but it is interesting as an example of the length to which states may go in protecting themselves from possible harmful action by interstate agencies: to put it differently, as an extreme example of the distrust states have felt of interstate agencies. Article VI of the Oil Compact makes any action of the Interstate Oil Compact Commission subject not only to the approval of a majority of the whole number of compacting states present at the meeting, but also to a possible second vote, this time on the basis of the amount of oil production in each state. The Compact provides that, in taking this "interest" vote, each state shall be counted "in the decimal proportion fixed by the ratio of its daily production during the preceding calendar half-year to the daily average production of all the compacting states during the same period." Such a vote would guarantee that the heavy producers could never be outvoted by the small and, as a matter of fact, would buttress Texas' commanding position in the oil industry. The realities of the oil business have caused the Commission to respect both the larger producers in general and Texas in particular, and the second vote provision has remained dormant. Like all interstate agencies, the Interstate Oil Compact Commission respects the states which make it up and renders formal controls to protect the states practically unnecessary.

Yet another means of control through prescription of procedure is the requirement found in a number of compacts that the meetings of the interstate commission shall be public. Like the usual provision that the agency's

books and records be open, this requirement assures the
states that the agency will not do secretly what it cannot
do openly. Virtually every interstate agency, however,
prides itself on its open meetings, not in dutiful response
to a compact, but because its chief power lies in its effect
on public opinion. Many compact agencies go to extreme lengths to publicize their meetings. Thus the requirement is actually not so much a control as a recognition of one of the effective means of interstate administration.

One or two compacts still further restrict interstate
agencies by prescribing patterns of operation. The
Pacific Marine Fisheries Compact, for example, requires
the commission it creates to confer with an advisory committee representing industry and other private interests
on any recommendation it desires to make for either
state or federal action.[16] Both the Atlantic and the Gulf
States Marine Fisheries Compacts provide that the
U.S. Fish and Wildlife Service shall perform the Commissions' research,[17] thus preventing them from developing strength in their own staffs. The Delaware River
Port Authority Compact requires that before the establishment of any facility is recommended to the legislatures, the Authority shall have demonstrated that existing
private facilities are inadequate.[18] And the compact
creating the Waterfront Commission of New York Harbor requires the Commission to demonstrate annually

[16] Article VII.
[17] Atlantic States Marine Fisheries Compact, Article VII;
Gulf States Marine Fisheries Compact, Article VII.
[18] Delaware River Compact, Article IV.

the "public necessity" of its several functions.[19] Presumably, if it found that such necessity no longer existed, the Commission would be expected to recommend the abolition of some or all of its functions.

Finally, the states may control compact agencies either by refusing to re-ratify a compact or by withdrawing from one. A relatively large number of compacts are ratified by the party states for limited periods, so that a state dissatisfied with the performance of the agency need simply fail to re-ratify before the date of expiration and thus end its participation. Secondly, since almost all of the compacts provide for the withdrawal of party states upon due notice, dissatisfied states may conveniently terminate their membership. It would seem that the privilege of re-ratification and of withdrawal might be effective means of controlling interstate bodies, since the mere threat to take either action would usually be enough to accomplish whatever reform a given state might desire. The force of these devices is conjectural, however; for neither has been used. Nothing illustrates so well the circumspection with which compact agencies have handled their relations with the states as the fact that not one has been rebuffed by states withdrawing or failing to re-ratify. A few of the interstate agencies have become inactive, but only because the need which they were created to meet ceased.

The operating-type interstate agencies have been subjected to more controls than the technical or recommendatory ones because they have been endowed with greater powers within their fields than most intra-state

[19] Article IV, section 13.

agencies enjoy. Like the other interstate agencies, they have done nothing to make extra restraints advisable. Nevertheless, the Port of New York Authority and the Delaware River Port Authority are restricted in several ways in addition to the sorts of controls ordinarily brought to bear on all compact agencies. Although both are empowered to acquire personal and real property for their facilities, both are prohibited from taking any property "vested in or held by [the party states], or by any county, city, borough, village, township, or other municipality . . . without the authority or consent of such . . . municipality. . . ." [20] The Delaware Compact goes a step further by declaring that the Authority may not construct, erect, or otherwise acquire "any new facility or project" until it has submitted a detailed report "dealing only with such contemplated facility or project" to the legislatures and governors of the party states and until the governors have filed with the commission written consents to proceed.[21] The laws of New York and New Jersey and the Delaware River Compact itself require that all highway and street approaches connecting the cities served by the bridges and tunnels of the Authority be agreed upon by the state and local highway officials concerned. Both authorities are further subject to revenue restrictions. By the terms of their compacts

[20] Port of New York Authority Compact, Article VI. Article V of the Delaware River Port Authority Compact virtually repeats this language except that the Delaware commission may take such property if "expressly authorized to do so by the Commonwealth or State in which such municipality or port district is located."

[21] Article XII.

or in accordance with statute, both must not only support themselves by tolls and other charges but must accumulate reserve funds to guarantee their bonds.

Despite many and ingenious restraints, the operating-type of compact agencies have frequently been attacked on the ground that they are not subject to "democratic controls." Critics of the New York Port Authority have charged that it "does not make its decisions to build another tunnel, or to expand an airport instead of investing in mass-transit facilities, in terms of the whole public, or of the interest of the whole area. . . . It makes its decisions in terms of its own, more limited public—*i.e.*, the auto driver who keeps it going with his tolls, and the bond market. The N. Y. P. A. . . . like many another authority, ostensibly 'nonpolitical,' has developed a politics of its own, a politics of specialists, who may or may not be responsive to the public interest." [22] The Authority may be extremely efficient, runs the charge, but it is hardly an instrument of democratic government.

In rebuttal, the New York Port Authority has repeatedly emphasized the degree to which it is subject to control by the states and thus indirectly by the people. Matthias E. Lukens, Assistant Executive Director of the Authority, lists six direct and eight indirect controls available to the states whenever they desire to apply them:

Direct	*Indirect*
1. Commissioners appointed by governors.	1. Annual reports required.
	2. Self-support required.

[22] "New Strength in City Hall," *Fortune*, LVI (November, 1957), 256.

2. Commissioners subject to removal by governors.
3. Commissioners' actions subject to veto by governors.
4. Statutory implementation of project planning required.
5. Municipal approval required in some cases.
6. Limitations imposed on use of revenue.

3. Auditing and examination required.
4. Authority is suable.
5. Tenants exercise certain controls.[23]
6. Municipal cooperation necessary.
7. Public records and community relations.
8. Necessity of financial solvency.[24]

Mr. Lukens feels that these controls are quite as many as the average political unit bears and that they are entirely adequate to protect the people.

Whereas the framers of interstate compacts have created an armory of negatively conceived controls upon interstate agencies, they have usually omitted to construct even the rudiments of a positive system of coordination between the states and the agencies. The fact is, however, that the development of coordination and cooperation is much more important than the exercise of restraint. Although for legal reasons and because of the influence of tradition compacts and the state laws ratifying them may be expected to retain the emphasis on control, positive relations between the compact agencies and the

[23] Mr. Lukens feels that since some of the Port Authority's tenants are private industries, they may leave if the Authority's policy as a landlord does not please them. Thus he argues that the tenants exercise a positive, though indirect, control over the Port Authority's policies.

[24] Matthias E. Lukens, in "The Port of New York Authority: A Case Study of an Interstate Mechanism," an address delivered before the American Political Science Association, Washington, D.C., September 12, 1953.

party states are slowly being developed. The pattern of these relations is far from established. They are still characteristically informal, but as their utility comes to be more widely recognized they will doubtless be regularized.

A number of kinds of contacts with compact agencies have been developed by the states. In some instances, the requirement of an annual report serves less as a means of control than of communication. Certainly to the extent that the reports are studied, they serve to inform legislators and executive officials about the activities of compact agencies. The best report can only summarize and generalize, however, so that, even if reports were widely distributed and read, they would be in themselves an inadequate channel of communication.

Much more effective is personal participation in compact activities by members of legislatures and intra-state agencies. Increasingly, legislators are being appointed members of interstate bodies; and a number of compacts and the laws ratifying compacts require the appointment of at least one legislator from each party state. In this way the legislatures may be linked directly with interstate agencies, and the legislative point of view may be expressed at every meeting of the compact body. When the legislative point of view is taken into account in the formulation of policy, legislative controls over the execution of policy become unnecessary. Similarly, the participation of state administrative officials, frequently as *ex officio* members, makes for smooth relations with the executive departments of state government.

Several legislatures have assigned committees in one or

both chambers some degree of responsibility for matters related to interstate compacts. In some states, standing committees on interstate cooperation[25] have been established, and a few of these have taken the lead in developing contacts with interstate agencies. None is specifically charged with this duty, however, and few even attempt to perform it. Most of these committees are concerned almost exclusively with proposals for the negotiation or ratification of interstate compacts rather than with developing relations with interstate agencies in operation. Other standing subject-matter committees concern themselves with compact activities from time to time. Their interest is usually incidental to other matters, however, and invariably temporary. Special committees are also employed occasionally by legislatures, as in Missouri, where the 69th General Assembly appointed an interim committee to study and report on the Bi-State Development Agency.

In addition, forty-eight states have now created permanent statutory bodies with authority in interstate relations, usually called the Commission on Interstate Cooperation, which have been mentioned above. These groups are typically composed of five members from the lower and five from the upper house of the legislature and five appointed by the governor. Usually, but not invariably, members of the standing committees on interstate cooperation automatically serve as the legislative members of the Commissions on Interstate Coopera-

[25] The nomenclature varies; these committees are called "Committee on Interstate Relations," "Committee on Interstate and Federal Relations," or "Committee on Federal and Interstate Cooperation."

tion. Such commissions, which are the god-children of the Council of State Governments, are uniformly charged by law with formulating proposals for interstate cooperation and with carrying on "negotiations with the purpose of adopting interstate compacts with other states." [26] Their authority generally stops at this point, so that they are little concerned with the execution of interstate compacts.

Although few of them are so used, the Commissions on Interstate Cooperation, as has been suggested, might provide a channel of communication between the legislatures and interstate agencies. New York's Joint Legislative Committee on Interstate Cooperation is perhaps the only one which has fully and consistently exploited this opportunity. It conceives as a part of its duties "keeping in touch with the interstate agencies and rendering what aid [it] can in interstate negotiations." [27] The Virginia Commission on Interstate Cooperation also lists as one of its functions the provision of "a means through which . . . Virginia may cooperate with other states in planning, developing and reviewing ideas, projects and programs of cooperation on problems with interstate implications, including appropriate interstate compacts or agreements. . . ." [28] This function does not seem, however, to be performed.

Several Commissions on Interstate Cooperation in-

[26] *Public Laws of Rhode Island,* ch. 660, sec. 201 (1939).

[27] Elisha T. Barrett, Chairman of the New York Joint Legislative Committee on Interstate Cooperation, to authors, August 1, 1957.

[28] Virginia Commission on Interstate Cooperation, *Annual Report* (1956), 9.

clude reports on the activities of interstate agencies in their annual reports to the legislatures, thus providing an additional source of information. In 1956, however, only eighteen Commissions submitted formal annual reports to the legislatures. For the most part, the Commissions feel that they have no "further obligations after an interstate compact has been ratified by [the] legislature." [29] In any case, few of them have permanent staff adequate for developing extensive relations with interstate agencies, and the members themselves are by the nature of their appointments primarily oriented in other directions. Although effective in other ways, these Commissions do not as yet serve as a permanent link between interstate compact agencies at work and their parent legislatures. Their potential in this respect is obviously great, however; and a number of them have indicated to the authors that they hope to develop it in the near future.

At least two legislatures have followed other methods of systematizing their relations with interstate compact agencies. In West Virginia, the Legislative Auditor's Office receives all correspondence and publications, including reports, from the compact agencies to which West Virginia is a party and transmits whatever it deems necessary to the appropriate legislative committees. And in Kentucky, all state agencies, including those founded upon interstate compacts, are required to submit copies of their reports, annual or otherwise, to the Legislative Research Commission, which may propose suitable legis-

[29] Everett T. Copenhaver, Chairman, Commission on Intergovernmental Cooperation of Wyoming, to authors, July 12, 1957.

lation for the consideration of the General Assembly.

In addition to their contacts with legislatures, interstate compact agencies have a variety of relations with state executive departments. Where the governor is a member of an interstate body, intimate contact is of course assured; and close relations have also developed where executive department officials serve as *ex officio* members of interstate agencies. The activities of virtually every compact agency involve at some point one or more of the departments of its constituent states. Several compacts even bind the states to furnish whatever help the interstate agencies may need from intrastate divisions. For example, the Sabine River Compact declares, "Each State shall provide such available facilities, supplies, equipment, technical information and other assistance as the Administration may require. . . . ." [30]

Generally speaking, there is thus much closer contact with and awareness of the interstate compact agencies in the executive than in the legislative branches of the states. In no state, however, has a single official or department been specifically charged with maintaining liaison with compact agencies. It is true that Texas has an Interstate Compact Commissioner with general authority to negotiate compacts in designated fields, but his function does not include maintenance of contact with established agencies. Several Western states have Interstate Streams Commissioners who work with interstate water apportionment agencies without, however, being

[30] Article VII, H.

concerned with the operations of compact agencies as such.

The numerous contacts between state executive departments and interstate compact agencies remain unilateral, not to say haphazard, despite the fact that it is a widely recognized "principle of sound administrative structure and legislative responsibility [that] some liaison should exist" between the states and the compact agencies to which they are parties.[31]

Even though interstate compacts are primarily aspects of state law and administration, they and the agencies they create are objects of federal concern as well. Both Congress and the federal executive branches have various kinds of relations with an increasing number of compact agencies, and of course litigation involving them may be adjudicated by the federal courts. As compact agencies assume more prominent roles in American government and public administration, the federal government may be expected to develop a coherent policy toward them and suitable devices for maintaining contact with them.

On the surface it would appear that the interest of Congress in interstate compacts is confined to their negotiation and ratification and that even there it is nominal. On one or two occasions, however, Congress has seemed to advocate the use of compacts by the states, for it has passed consent-in-advance legislation for compacts devoted to forest conservation and civil defense. On the other hand, it has not acted on the pleas of many groups

[31] Donald C. Simpson, Executive Secretary, Legislative Council, State of Washington, to authors, July 11, 1957.

that it enact general consent-in-advance legislation. One such plea was that of the 43rd Annual Governors Conference, which resolved that Congress enact general consent-in-advance legislation permitting the states to negotiate compacts providing for interstate cooperation in unspecified "fields of action for which the States have primary responsibility under our Federal Constitution." [32] Each compact presents a different set of circumstances, and Congress has been reluctant to surrender its power to consider it particularly. Moreover, it hesitates to become an advocate in an area where the initiative properly lies with the states.

Accordingly, Congress has confined itself pretty much to facilitating the approval and ratification of compacts; yet in recent years it has begun to show a more active interest in the interstate compacts and agencies devoted to the conservation and apportionment of waters. The federal government has participated in the work carried on under nine compacts of this description. In every case, Congress regularly appropriates funds to help meet the operating costs of the agencies in question.

Like the states, Congress tends to assert its rights and to include devices intended to protect the federal interest from possible actions of interstate agencies. Often it contents itself with specific retention of the right to alter, amend, or repeal the resolution or statute by which it consents to a compact. This kind of provision might be regarded as a means of ultimate control over operations under compacts, but Congress has never so used it. Recently, indeed, Congress has suggested that the possibility

[32] Cf. *State Government*, XXIV (November, 1951), 286.

that it should ever exercise this right is extremely remote, at least in connection with the water allocation compacts. After the sentence reserving the right to repeal its consenting act, Congress has added in three instances the following statement: "This reservation shall not be construed to prevent the vesting of rights to the use of water pursuant to applicable law, and no alteration, amendment or repeal of Section 1 of this Act [i. e., of the compact itself] shall be held to affect rights so vested." [33] It would seem that the existence of explicitly affirmed vested rights would prevent Congress from lightly removing the basis on which such rights are built.

In some cases, Congress has taken a slightly different line. In the statute consenting to the New England Interstate Water Pollution Control Compact, for example, it provided that "Nothing contained in this act or in the compact herein approved shall be construed as impairing or affecting the sovereignty of the United States or any of its rights or jurisdiction in and over the area or waters which are subject to the compact." [34] Similar language appears in all compacts involving navigable interstate waters, in which of course the federal government has a constitutional interest. This sort of provision is also no doubt a formality, for any encroachment on the federal sovereignty by a compact agency would certainly be dealt with by negotiation between the agency and federal officials long before it could be regarded as dangerous.

[33] The Yellowstone River Compact, 65 Stat. 663 (1951); the Canadian River Compact, 66 Stat. 74 (1952); and the Sabine River Compact, 68 Stat. 690 (1954).

[34] 61 Stat. 612 (1947).

On two occasions, Congress has given only limited consent to compacts. Although the Atlantic States Marine Fisheries Compact provided that "this compact shall continue in force and remain binding upon each compacting state until renounced by it," [35] Congress, upon the recommendation of the House Committee on Merchant Marine and Fisheries, limited its consent to fifteen years. Unless extended by affirmative action of Congress within this period, the Compact would be terminated. The Committee seemed to feel that by this means Congress could evaluate the work of the Atlantic States Marine Fisheries Commission before renewing its approval. The provision was repealed in 1950 and no similar one has been made with respect to other compacts. To have retained it and to have broadened the use of such measures would not only have prevented the agencies created by compact from becoming permanent but would also have forced Congress, or the affected committees, into regular evaluative procedures for which it is not suited.

Congress had given only limited approval to the Interstate Compact to Conserve Oil and Gas in 1935. Approval was given subject to reconsideration after two years; later the period was extended to four years, the current extension being effective until September 1, 1959. There is little doubt that Congress distrusted the motives of the compacting states in 1935 or that it distrusts the Interstate Oil Compact Commission today. Congress seems to fear that the Commission is a front for a price-fixing arrangement among the oil-producing states for

[35] Article XII.

the benefit of the major oil-producing companies and that it is a threat to the Congressional authority to regulate interstate commerce.[36] When the Compact was last up for renewal, this fear was strong enough to cause Congress to impose an additional control of a kind never before brought to bear on an interstate agency in operation.

An amendment to the joint resolution by which Congress renewed its approval of the Compact provided that for the next four years the Attorney General of the United States should make an annual report to Congress as to whether in his opinion the activities of the Commission had resulted in "the stabilizing or fixing of prices of oil or gas, the creation or perpetuation of any monopoly, or the promotion of any regimentation in the production or sale of oil or gas; with the understanding that conservation and the protection of the small producer are the paramount purposes of any rules and regulations issued under the Compact."[37] Thus the Oil Commission has been placed under surveillance to prevent violation of the anti-trust laws. So far, the Attorney General has made three reports.[38] No evidence of any of the activities Congress feared has been presented; in

[36] See the remarks of counsel to U.S. Senate Interior and Insular Affairs Committee at meeting of Interstate Oil Compact Commission in Billings, Montana, in 1953, quoted in *The Interstate Oil Quarterly Bulletin*, XII (September, 1953), 12.

[37] Senate Joint Resolution 38, 84th Congress, 1st Session (1955).

[38] *Report of the Attorney General Pursuant to Section 2 of the Joint Resolution of July 28, 1955* . . . , September 1, 1956; *Second Report* . . . , September 1, 1957; *Third Report* . . . , September 1, 1958.

fact, the reports have been unqualified endorsements of the motives and methods of the Commission.

One other method of controlling interstate agencies which Congress has used is exemplified in the restriction placed upon the Bi-State Development Agency in the joint resolution consenting to the Compact which creates it. Article III, section 8, of this Compact provides that the Agency shall have, among others, the power "to exercise such additional powers as shall be conferred on it by the legislature of either state concurred in by the legislature of the other or by act of Congress." In the consent resolution Congress reiterated the point that no power or powers may be exercised under the grant "unless and until such power or powers . . . shall have been approved by an Act of Congress." [39] Although Congress probably has the power in any case to reject an additional grant of power to a compact agency, its unequivocal assertion in this instance leaves no doubt at all that the agency may not go beyond the powers originally delegated by the compact without Congressional review and consent.

In addition to the devices mentioned, Congress further controls, or at least enlarges the possibility of controlling, interstate agencies by requiring, as the states do, annual reports. The only agencies of whom reports have been required are the Atlantic States Marine Fisheries Commission and the Pacific Marine Fisheries Commission. The suggestion originated in the House Committee on Merchant Marine and Fisheries and is expressed as follows in the act consenting to the Atlantic Compact:

[39] 64 Stat. 568 (1950).

Relations with State and Federal Governments

"The Atlantic States Marine Fisheries Commission . . . shall make an annual report to Congress not later than 60 days after the beginning of each regular session thereof. Such report shall set forth the activities of the Commission during the calendar year ending immediately prior to the beginning of such session." [40]

The Pacific Commission must meet substantially the same requirement.[41] Congress has of course a direct interest in fisheries and so wishes to be kept informed of interstate compact agencies operating in this area. It is significant, however, that no similar requirement was made of the Gulf States Marine Fisheries Commission nor of any compact agencies operating in other areas where the federal government has equally legitimate concerns. Although both Commissions have faithfully submitted the required reports, there is no evidence that they have been used by individual members of Congress, by the Committee on Merchant Marine and Fisheries, or by Congress as a whole.

Perhaps Congress has been inconsistent in its treatment of compact agencies because it has not developed a single concept on which to base its dealings with them and, consequently, has created no machinery for the purpose. Although Rule XI of the House of Representatives assigns regular, continuing responsibility for compacts to three committees, none of them regards the assignment as implying anything beyond handling the routine of Congressional approval. The Committee on the Judiciary is responsible for compacts in general; the Committee on Interstate and Foreign Commerce for the

[40] 56 Stat. 267 (1942).   [41] See 61 Stat. 419 (1947).

Interstate Oil Compact; and the Committee on Interior and Insular Affairs for compacts relating to apportionment of waters. In addition, the Committee on Merchant Marine and Fisheries and the Committee on Public Works are concerned with the interstate agencies whose activities touch their fields.

A similar situation prevails in the Senate, where Rule XXV assigns responsibility for compacts in general to the Committee on the Judiciary and for water allocation compacts to the Committee on Interior and Insular Affairs. Neither of these nor any of the Senate counterparts of the other House committees which by the nature of their subjects are more or less involved with compacts has ever developed a procedure for keeping informed about the activities of interstate agencies.

Thus in neither house is there a central point of contact for compact agencies, and, as has been noted, they are only rarely required to report to Congress. The relations of Congress to these agencies are therefore casual and its knowledge of their activities fragmentary. Presumably some members of Congress have, from time to time, some contact with members of interstate compact agencies or their staffs; but short of changing its present organizational pattern, which Congress notoriously does not like to do, Congress is unlikely to develop any very positive, consistent attitudes toward compacts and the agencies they establish.

Among the executive agencies of the federal government, relations with compact agencies have been much more nearly regularized. Executive departments are now commonly brought into the picture even during the period in which Congress considers its consent to a compact. The Congressional committee to which a compact is referred often sends it to the executive agencies concerned with the subject matter for comment. Thus, during the first session of the 85th Congress, the draft of the Little Missouri River Compact was sent to both the Department of the Interior and to the Department of the Army, and the proposed Merrimack River Flood Control Compact was sent to the Department of the Army. In both instances, the committees postponed action until replies had been received. Although the committees of Congress are not bound by the recommendations so obtained, they are no doubt influenced by departmental comment not only on compacts but on the functions and powers of the proposed agencies.[42] The Bureau of the Budget is also frequently asked for the viewpoint of the administration on proposed compacts. The Assistant Director has become an informal source of information about compacts for officials within the administration.

Once compacts are approved and ratified and the agencies they create begin operations, direct relations between them and the executive departments of the federal government become common. Usually, the emphasis of the executive departments is on cooperation rather than control, and many of them work closely with compact agencies. On the water apportionment and the stream pollution commissions, federal representatives appointed by the President serve as members and in most cases as

[42] See House Reports No. 948 and 334, 85th Congress, 1st Session (1957).

chairmen. Since they are employees of federal departments concerned with the same matters as the interstate
agencies, they make a link between these bodies and the
federal government which is very effective. Even where
this particular arrangement is missing, compact agencies
have developed modes of communication with the federal government which are almost as valuable. For example, the Yellowstone River Compact declares, "The
Secretary of the Army; the Secretary of the Interior; the
Secretary of Agriculture; the Chairman, Federal Power
Commission; the Secretary of Commerce; and such other
Federal officers . . . having services or data useful or
necessary to the Compact Commission, shall cooperate
. . . with the Commission in the execution of its duty
. . . ";[43] and the annual reports of the Commission
testify to the help which these officials give.

The Atlantic States and the Gulf States Marine Fisheries Compacts are even more explicit about the services
federal officials shall perform for the commissions. They
provide that the U.S. Fish and Wildlife Service of the
Department of the Interior shall be their primary research agency. In both cases, the years have brought
"an increasingly close liaison between [the commissions]
and the Fish and Wildlife Service. . . ." [44] Neither commission asks the Service for research which states party to
the Compacts can do themselves; instead, they "ask
primarily for studies involving species of interstate sig-

[43] Article III, D.
[44] Wayne D. Heydecker, Secretary-Treasurer, Atlantic States
Marine Fisheries Commission, to Richard H. Leach, July 15,
1954.

nificance and wide range or off-shore research or work of a character that . . . requires integration of data along the whole range of a species." [45] Both commissions and the Fish and Wildlife Service are pleased with this arrangement and feel that it has resulted in greater advancement than could have been brought about by the three agencies working severally.

Although the Rio Grande, the Pecos, the Yellowstone, and the Sabine River Compacts do not provide the arrangement, the commissions they established have contracted with the U.S. Geological Survey to operate gaging stations at points on the rivers and to compile data required in the administration of the compacts. The Upper Colorado River Commission, which has no such formal relation with the Survey, nevertheless relies upon it heavily for data essential to its operations.

The water allocation and stream pollution compact commissions, working as they do in fields of immediate concern to the federal government, have developed the most nearly consistent patterns of relations, but other compact agencies have also come to depend on various forms of federal help. Even the Southern Regional Education Board—the Compact establishing which was not approved by Congress because it felt that education was not a subject of federal interest—has founded one of its most extensive programs, that in mental health, on a grant from the National Institute of Mental Health. When the Western Interstate Commission for Higher Education wished to study dental educational facilities in relation to dental manpower requirements in the

[45] *Ibid.*

West, it turned to the Division of Dental Resources of the U.S. Public Health Service for assistance. The survey lasted eighteen months and resulted in the formulation of a new program by the Commission. The Interstate Oil Compact Commission not only benefits from the enforcement of the "Connally Hot Oil Act," which supports state conservation laws by prohibiting the shipment in interstate commerce of oil produced in excess of that allowed by the state regulatory agencies, but receives much valuable assistance in its own work from such federal agencies as the Department of the Interior and the Federal Power Commission.

This analysis of the relations between the agencies established by interstate compact and their parent states on the one hand and the federal government on the other reveals that a distinct constitutional evolution has occurred. As might be expected, the older kinds of governmental unit have tended to regard the newer with hostility and suspicion which are obviously reflected in the language of the compacts and related legislation, although some of this language may be merely the expression of caution or tradition. Time and experience, however, have shown that the compact agencies are not rivals but partners in pursuit of some of the same objectives which the older units are seeking. Furthermore, it begins to be apparent that the compact agencies can do new kinds of work hitherto inhibited by adventitious physical and administrative boundaries and that in so doing these agencies preserve for the states functions which might otherwise go by default to the federal government or lapse. As these aspects of interstate compact agencies become more widely appreciated, they may overcome the effects of the fact that compacts are still "the tools of states jealous of their prerogatives and niggardly in their grants of authority." [46] The impressive accommodations already reached by informal means seem to be having their effect upon the tone of statutes and compacts. Most important of all, the interstate agencies exist, they function, they begin to have a history; however negative the tone of statutes and compacts, they have produced a positive development in American government.

[46] Howard W. Odum and Harry E. Moore, *American Regionalism* (New York, 1938), 206.

3: Interstate Compact Agencies:

Powers and Personnel

The administrative agencies created by interstate compacts are variously called *authorities, commissions, administrations, boards,* and *agencies.* The word chosen in each case does not seem to imply a difference in the agency's functions or powers; instead, it probably reflects simply the personal preference of the framers of the particular compact. At any rate, no legal differences correspond to those of nomenclature. The compacts also vary in prescribing the membership of the agencies they create. Some consist of a single representative from each party state, whereas a few are composed of as many as six or eight from each state; three members from each state is perhaps the most common arrangement. Where the number is smaller the compact is universally in a specialized area—such as water apportionment, oil conservation, or waterfront crime control—where technical competence or special administrative skill is the prime requisite for membership. Greater representation is necessary if the compact deals with a broader area of public policy—such as fishery conservation, education, or control of water pollution—where a number of different points of view in each party state must be taken into account. Where interests of the United States are involved, provision is usually made for the representation without voting privileges of the federal government. With only one exception each state party to a compact is allotted the same number of representatives.[1]

The compacts also take a number of approaches to the qualifications required for membership in the interstate agencies. About half do not require the states to designate any particular individuals or types of individuals, permitting the members instead to be "designated or appointed in accordance with the laws of each state." [2] Some add the proviso that the persons appointed must be citizens or resident voters of the states from which they are appointed. At the other extreme, three compacts specifically designate either individuals or the group from which they must be chosen. Thus the New England Water Pollution Control Compact provides that one commissioner from each state shall be a representative of the state health department; one, a representative of the state water pollution control agency; one, a representative of municipal interests; one, a representative of industrial interests; and the fifth, a representative of a state agency "acting for fisheries or conservation." [3] The Atlantic and

---

[1] The Pacific Marine Fisheries Compact allots Washington only one member and California and Oregon both three.
[2] Canadian River Compact, Article X, a.   [3] Article III.

Gulf States Marine Fisheries Compacts provide that the executive officer or administrative head of the state agency charged with the conservation of fisheries resources shall be one member from each state and that of the other two, one shall be a member of the legislature and the other a "citizen who shall have a knowledge of and interest in the marine fisheries problem. . . ." [4] Several compacts include different provisions for members from different party states. The Sabine River Compact, for example, names as the members of the Sabine River Compact Administration from Louisiana the Director of the Louisiana Department of Public Works and a citizen of the Sabine watershed; but it permits the two Texas commissioners to be appointed by the governor of Texas without restriction.[5] Similarly, and perhaps because Texas is a party state there too, the Rio Grande Compact specifies that the State Engineers of Colorado and New Mexico serve as commissioners from those states but provides that "the Commissioner from Texas shall be appointed by the governor of Texas." [6]

A number of compacts specify who some of the commissioners from each state shall be but leave the choice of the rest of each state's delegation to the discretion of the states themselves. Thus the Southern Regional Education Compact provides that the governor of each state shall serve *ex officio* on the Southern Regional Education Board, along with four citizens whom he shall appoint,

[4] Atlantic and Gulf States Marine Fisheries Compacts, Article III.
[5] Sabine River Compact, Article VII, c.
[6] Rio Grande Compact, Article XII.

of whom at least one must be from the field of education and at least one a legislator. Finally, a small group of compacts designates where some or all of the commission members shall live instead of who they shall be. The Arkansas River Compact, for example, requires two of the three Colorado members to be residents and water right owners in particular water districts in the Arkansas River Valley and two of the Kansas members to be residents of particular counties.[7]

The provisions of compacts are not, however, always the last word on membership. In a number of cases where the party states are allowed to exercise discretion by the terms of the compact, conventions have grown up that limit in practice the sorts of persons who are appointed. Although the Southern Regional Education Compact, for example, calls simply for the appointment of four citizens, one of whom must be from the field of education and one from the legislature, the convention has come to be that the others are usually the president of the state university or university system, the president of the state land grant college, or the president of a state Negro institution.

The state legislatures often impose requirements in addition to those in the compact. As noted above, the majority of the compacts make no specification at all as to membership on the agencies they establish, leaving the matter wholly up to the states. In the acts ratifying such compacts, the legislatures have frequently imposed requirements of their own. The legislature of New Hampshire, for example, in ratifying the New England Higher

[7] Arkansas River Compact, Article VIII, c.

Education Compact, which declares that the three members of the New England Board of Higher Education from each state shall be appointed by the governor thereof and places no limitations on him, restricted the governor of New Hampshire in making his appointments to the Board by saying that one commissioner shall always be the president of the state university and one a member of the state legislature.[8] The Vermont legislature made identical provisions in the act by which it ratified the same Compact. Examples of this kind of legislative intervention are legion. Such statutes may be enacted at the time of ratification or at any subsequent time.

The legislatures may also choose to ignore a compact's prescriptions as to commission membership. The New England Interstate Water Pollution Control Compact, it will be recalled, laid down a general pattern for the appointment of commissioners; and, although the Compact does go on to say that "where a state in its enabling legislation decides that [its] best interest . . . will be otherwise served" by following a different pattern, it may do so,[9] the intent of the framers of the Compact to assure a broad and balanced representation on the Commission is very clear. The New Hampshire legislature, however, disregarded the last three parts of the recommended procedure (namely, that those members should be representative of municipal interests, industrial interests, and the state agency acting for fisheries and con-

[8] *New Hampshire Laws* (1955), ch. 232, sec. 3.
[9] New England Interstate Water Pollution Control Compact, Article III.

servation) and directed the governor instead to designate as commissioners three members of the New Hampshire Water Pollution Commission, one of whom must be the chairman.[10] New York did the same thing. Her enabling legislation for the Compact states: "The state shall be represented by five commissioners to be appointed by the governor. One shall be the commissioner of health, one . . . a member of the water pollution control board and the others shall be such persons as the governor shall determine will serve the best interests of the state." [11] Again, there can be no question of the propriety of New York's action. The purpose the framers of the Compact hoped to achieve may thus have been altered, however, and perhaps the very nature of the commission they hoped to establish changed beyond description.

Although it is common practice in compacts to make state officials *ex officio* members of interstate commissions—indeed, a number of compacts carefully provide that "nothing herein shall prevent the appointment of an officer or employee of any State or the United States Government to membership" [12]—the result is often the delegation by the designated official of his role to a subordinate. In fact, state laws ratifying compacts often recognize the necessity for such delegation. The Mississippi statute ratifying the Gulf States Marine Fisheries Compact, for instance, permits the President of the state Seafood Commission, who is named as an *ex officio* mem-

[10] *New Hampshire Laws* (1951), ch. 190, sec. 3.
[11] *Laws of New York*, 172nd Session (1949), ch. 764, sec. 4.
[12] The wording of the Ohio River Valley Water Sanitation Compact, Article IV.

ber of the Gulf States Marine Fisheries Commission, to "delegate, from time to time, to any deputy or other member of the . . . Seafood Commission, the power to be present and participate, including voting, as his representative or substitute at any meeting of or hearing by or other proceeding of the [Gulf States] Commission." [13] Thus the advantage of having the President of the Commission serve—to link the state department most directly concerned with fisheries through its executive officer to the activities of the Compact Commission—may be lost before it can ever be felt. The reason for permitting such delegations is obvious; consequently, the choice of state officials as *ex officio* members of compact commissions may not be a wise policy in the first place. The state officials most often selected by the compacts or by the state legislatures to represent states on an interstate agency are high-ranking people—governors, heads of executive departments, directors of agencies—whose responsibilities within the state constitute a heavy burden in themselves. The State Commissioner of Health in New York, for example, has so important and responsible a job that effective service on the New England Interstate Water Pollution Control Commission is virtually impossible for him, even if he wishes to make a significant contribution to its activities. The same thing is true of governors, state engineers, and the other state officers who are usually named as compact commissioners. By the very nature of their full-time jobs, they are part-time compact commissioners, if that.

From time to time and in exceptional circumstances

[13] *General Laws of Mississippi* (1950), ch. 556, sec. 2.

these limitations are overcome. Thus the governors, at least those from oil-producing states, play an impertant role in the business of the Interstate Oil Compact Commission.[14] But across the board the results obtained from employing such *ex officio* commissioners have not been impressive. When it is realized that often the same state official is made an *ex officio* member of two or three compact commissions at the same time—the State Engineer of New Mexico, for one, serves on three—the improbability of obtaining good results seems even greater.

The purpose aimed at in appointing *ex officio* members can perhaps be better served by another device being incorporated in more recent compacts. They call for the appointment of a subordinate official, who assumes, as a part of his regular state job, responsibility for liaison with the compact commission. As has been noted, the New England Interstate Water Pollution Control Compact provides that each state shall name "a representative," who need not be the administrative head, of the state health department and the state water pollution control agency; and the Pacific Marine Fisheries Compact permits "an officer of the state agency charged with fishery conservation" to be appointed to the Pacific Marine Fisheries Commission by California.[15] Thus the interests of the regular state agencies most closely related to activity under the compacts are represented on the compact

[14] See Richard H. Leach, "The Interstate Oil Compact: A Study in Success," *Oklahoma Law Review*, X (August, 1957), 274–88.
[15] Pacific Marine Fisheries Compact, Article III.

agencies without imposing an impossible burden on an already fully occupied higher official.

For the most part compacts do not spell out how commissioners shall be appointed. Uniformly, the party states have vested the power to appoint in the governor. Since in about half the cases, however, the persons who may be appointed to compact commissions are specifically designated either by title or general description in the compact or in subsequent state law, the governor's discretion in appointment is limited. Even in the other half, the governor's power is often limited by the requirement that the appointment be made by and with the advice and consent of the state legislature,[16] the state senate,[17] or the governor's council.[18] In one case a governor is prohibited from appointing more than two members from the same political party,[19] but this restriction is more apparent than real since in practice most appointments to interstate agencies are non-political.

[16] The Connecticut law ratifying the New England Higher Education Compact provides that members of the Board from Connecticut shall be appointed by the governor with the advice and consent of the General Assembly. (Connecticut Public Act 48, Special Session, 1955).

[17] Article II of the Palisades Interstate Park Compact provides that commissioners from the two states shall be appointed by the governors with the approval of the two state senates. The New Jersey law ratifying the Delaware River Compact makes the same provision with regard to the New Jersey members of the Delaware River Port Authority. (*New Jersey R.S., 1951–52 Supp.*, 32:20–11).

[18] The New Hampshire members of the Maine-New Hampshire Interstate Bridge Authority are appointed by "governor and Council." (*New Hampshire RSA 258* (1936)).

[19] The governor of New Hampshire to the Maine-New Hampshire Interstate Bridge Authority. *Ibid.*

When the United States participates in a compact program, the appointment of the United States representatives on the commission is, with one exception, made by the President. The exception was protested, however, and it is doubtful if another compact attempting to vest appointment in an officer other than the President will ever be approved by Congress. By the terms of the Yellowstone River Compact of 1950 the U.S. member is appointed by the Director of the U.S. Geological Survey.[20] Although the bond between the Survey and the Yellowstone River Compact Commission is close—as it is between the Survey and all the water allocation commissions—the Director of the Bureau of the Budget, to whom the Compact was referred for comment before it was approved by Congress, objected on the ground that the United States member should represent the interests of the national government as a whole, not those of a single agency. In a memorandum to President Truman, the Director of the Bureau declared that the provision of the Compact in question "was at variance with sound principles of Federal administration" and urged that the Yellowstone Compact not be regarded as a precedent for future compacts.[21] The objection seems to be well taken and no attempt has since been made to follow the Yellowstone pattern.

There is also a great deal of variation among compacts in regard to the terms members of the interstate bodies

[20] Yellowstone River Compact, Article III, A.
[21] *Documents on Use and Control of the Waters of Interstate and International Streams—Compacts, Treaties and Adjudications* (Washington, 1956), 246.

shall serve. The majority either specify that the term shall be set by the laws of the party states or do not mention a term at all, the result being the same. Legislatures usually set a term of three or four years, while the few compacts which themselves set the term tend to make them a little longer, ranging from three to six years.[22] All the latter, save one, set the same length of term for the members from all the party states. The Sabine River Compact alone makes a distinction between the terms to be served, the Texas member serving two years and the Louisiana member four.[23] Of course, where state officials serve *ex officio*, their terms run with their occupancy of their state offices. In almost every case the several terms are staggered so that most of the agencies are assured of a continuing nucleus of members. This arrangement and the fact that the average term is three years or longer, combine to give compact agencies considerable stability, which is probably essential in the light of the complexity of the problems with which most of them are concerned.

Finally, compacts differ greatly with respect to the compensation of the members of the bodies they establish. Only one stipulates the compensation: the Lake

[22] The members of the Waterfront Commission of New York Harbor serve three year terms; of the Arkansas River Compact Administration and the Southern Regional Education Board, four years; of the Tennessee-Missouri Bridge Commission, the Bi-State Development Agency, and the Delaware River Port Authority, five years; and of the Port of New York Authority, six years.

[23] Sabine River Compact, Article VII, c.

Champlain Bridge Compact requires that the "members
of the Commission shall each receive as compensation
for their services the sum of $10 a day for each day's
services performed. . . ." [24] Seven compacts [25] prohibit
compensation altogether. "No member of the Commission," declares the Palisades Interstate Park Compact,
"shall receive any compensation for his services as a
member" of the Commission. [26] Such provisions usually
reflect the feeling that members should serve, as Austin
Tobin, Executive Director of the Port of New York
Authority, has said, solely "for the satisfaction of rendering a constructive public service." The men who make
good commissioners, Tobin feels, "are men who would
not be attracted to the service by any monetary consideration" anyhow. [27] Thirteen compacts do not mention
compensation. In most of these cases, the states seem
to have taken the silence of the compact as an implied
injunction against compensation and have not acted to
provide for it. Some legislatures, in the absence of a
specific prohibition in a compact, have even supplied one
of their own in the legislation ratifying that particular
compact. Thus the Connecticut statute ratifying the
Northeastern Interstate Forest Fire Protection Compact
declares, "The commissioners . . . appointed shall be

[24] Lake Champlain Bridge Compact, Article IV.
[25] The Interstate Compact on the Potomac River Basin, the
Delaware River Compact, the Western Interstate Compact on
Higher Education, the Palisades Interstate Park Compact, the
Interstate Sanitation Compact, the Breaks Interstate Park Compact, and the Ohio River Valley Water Sanitation Compact.
[26] Palisades Interstate Park Compact, Article II.
[27] *The Daily Bond Buyer* (October 7, 1952), 5.

paid no compensation" [28] and the New Hampshire legislation follows suit. Other states, however, party to some of the same compacts, have provided for compensation. Massachusetts, for example, also a party to the Northeastern Forest Fire Protection Compact, grants to the representative on the Northeastern Forest Fire Protection Commission who is appointed by the governor (the other two members are salaried state officials who serve *ex officio*) $30 per day for his services on the Commission up to a limit of $600 per year. And Texas has provided payment of $15 per day to her representatives on the Sabine River Compact Administration.

There is as much variation even among the eleven compacts which do not themselves prohibit compensation. Eight seem to assume that the commissioners will be salaried. The Rio Grande Compact, for example, states that "The salaries and personal expenses of the Rio Grande Compact Commissioners for the three States shall be paid by their respective States . . . ";[29] and the Connecticut River Valley Flood Control Compact reads, "The compensation of members of the commission shall be fixed, determined and paid by the state which they respectively represent." [30] Neither Compact in so many words obligates the legislatures to pay the commissioners, but the expectation seems to be strong that they will. The states have in general responded by providing at

[28] *General Statutes of Connecticut* (*1949 Supplement*), Title 24, ch. 164 b., sec. 397 a.
[29] Rio Grande Compact, Article XII.
[30] Connecticut River Valley Flood Control Compact, Article II.

least token payments for their representatives. Two of the eleven compacts seem much less positive. Both the Arkansas and Sabine River Compacts contain a note of doubt that the commissioners will be paid: "The salaries, if any, and the personal expenses of each member shall be paid by the government he represents." [31] In fact, however, the states party to both Compacts have provided for compensation.

Not only is there great variation with regard to compensation among states; often within a single state no uniform pattern is followed. Texas pays its commissioners on the Sabine River Compact Administration $15 per day and expenses, but pays expenses only for its representatives on the Rio Grande and Pecos Commissions, the Gulf States Marine Fisheries Commission, and the Southern Regional Education Board. Vermont pays each member of the Connecticut River Valley Flood Control Commission $15 per day for their services, while its members on the Lake Champlain Bridge Commission receive only $10 a day and its members on the New England Board of Higher Education no compensation at all. And Massachusetts provides for the members of the Connecticut River Valley Flood Control Commission and New England Board of Higher Education who do not serve *ex officio* the same $30-a-day compensation it does for the appointed member of the Northeastern Forest Fire Protection Commission. But where the forest fire commissioner is limited to $600 a year, the limit set for the member of the Board of Higher Education is $2000 per year

[31] Arkansas River Compact, Article VIII, E, 1; Sabine River Compact, Article VII, k.

and no limit at all is imposed on the member of the Flood Control Commission. States do not seem to have evolved a consistent policy toward the use of compact commissioners which would help them solve such problems as compensation. Thus each case is treated separately and left to the pressures of the moment, and the result is great variation in state policy from one compact to another, which is reflected not only in regard to compensation but far deeper in the very nature of the bodies established by compact.

The Waterfront Commission of New York Harbor must be treated separately in this respect. It is a two-man commission, the commissioners themselves actually administering the provisions of the Compact. The framers of the Compact resolved that the "members representing each state . . . shall receive compensation to be fixed by the governor of such state." [32] The governors of both New York and New Jersey have agreed on a yearly salary of $17,500 for each commissioner. These two are the only compact commissioners in the United States who receive a salary commensurate with those of the officials at the head of other state agencies.

As the habit of providing, at the most, nominal compensation suggests, the position of a member of a compact agency is among the least recognized public positions in the United States. Altogether, there are only about 455 such officials in the nation. Although many of them are locally well known and a few have won national renown, it is in virtually every case because they hold or have held more conventional state or local office or

[32] Waterfront Commission Compact, Article III, 2.

because they have become prominent in local or national business or education circles and not because of their compact activities. Yet to say this is to say a great deal, for it clearly demonstrates that most compact officials are men who have achieved at least some measure of distinction in their particular fields.

So far as the authors know, the probity of members of the bodies founded on interstate compacts has been in question only once. Three former members of the Delaware River Joint Toll Bridge Commission were ordered on October 14, 1957, by a Bucks County, Pennsylvania, court to stand trial for alleged mishandling of funds.[33] The case has not yet been argued, but it is of interest here to note that the court action followed an investigation of the Commission by Governor George M. Leader of Pennsylvania and Governor Robert B. Meyner of New Jersey, suggesting that effective methods of control were available.[34] With this unfortunate exception, however, what has been said of the Interstate Sanitation Commission applies equally to most members of the compact agencies: "They are men who have risen to the top in their respective walks of life, banking, the law, teaching, research, real estate, science, the press and government. Some have served in their state legislatures, others have headed municipalities in the area. [Thus they are men] who know and understand the problems which follow each one of their decisions." [35]

[33] New York *Times* (October 15, 1957), 22.
[34] *Ibid.* (September 6, 1956), 52.
[35] Interstate Sanitation Commission, *Cleaning Up the Doorway to America, 20 Years of Progress in Pollution Control, 1936–1956* (1956), 5.

There is little evidence that political factors have been at all important in the selection of compact officials. Compact agencies do not entice the narrowly political man. The facts that the great majority of compact commissioners serve without compensation or with very little, that they have no direct channels to the voting public, and that what they can do is so hemmed in by a variety of state controls, have made appointment uninteresting and unattractive to the average politician. Thus where governors have been left free to appoint at their discretion, they have not generally relied on political criteria to guide them. Instead they have drawn upon men with at least a general understanding of the problems involved in the work under each compact. Because partisanship has not seriously affected appointments, there is a high rate of reappointment, assuring a nucleus of experienced members. Death and resignation are more common causes of change in personnel than failure to be reappointed.

The type of person appointed differs somewhat according to the type of agency involved. Members of the operating agencies are generally not required to be state officials serving *ex officio* (the Delaware River Port Authority is an exception—two of Pennsylvania's representatives are *ex officio*); thus the governors are freer in appointing commissioners. Because the tradition has developed that such bodies are similar in function to the board of directors of a major private corporation, the tendency is to appoint business executives. The members of the Port of New York Authority in 1957 included the chairman of the board of one of the nation's largest banks, the presidents of a large construction company and a paper company, two corporation lawyers, and a consulting engineer. All were men who in the course of their business lives are very much concerned with the problems of the industrial complex of which the Port of New York is the nexus. The majority of the members of the Delaware River Port Authority are similarly involved in the business activities of the Philadelphia-Camden area. The president of the Budd Company is one member of that Authority, for example. The more limited operating commissions do not, of course, draw so heavily from the ranks of well-known figures. The members of the Maine-New Hampshire Interstate Bridge Authority, the Lake Champlain Bridge Commission, and the Tennessee-Missouri Bridge Commission must be, under terms of the Compacts, residents of counties adjacent to the bridges. But the men appointed have all been leading citizens of these localities.

The members of the study-recommendatory agencies are not nearly so true to a single type as the members of the port authorities. They tend to vary according to the subject of the particular compact, both because *ex officio* members are more common and because of the specialized nature of the compacts. Thus educators predominate in the membership of the three higher education agencies; and, by the terms of the Compacts themselves, the majority of the members of the three fishery compact commissions are necessarily persons directly involved in the fishery industry. The Interstate Oil Compact Commission, aside from the governors, consists of experts in oil law, petroleum engineering, or oil conservation and production regulation. The members of the seven water apportionment agencies are perhaps the most specialized of all. Water use and water law are very technical subjects, with the result that water compact commissioners are to a man technical experts.

Although virtually every compact endows the agency it creates with the power to adopt its own rules for internal operation, most limit that grant of power by specifying the election of a minimum number of officers and requiring the observance of a few basic rules of procedure. Most frequently the compact requires that the members shall elect from their own number a chairman and a vice-chairman and permits the election or appointment of such other officers as the group shall deem necessary. The water compacts provide that the United States representative shall serve as chairman without the power to vote.[36] Some compacts provide in addition that a secretary (clerk), a secretary-treasurer, or a treasurer may be elected, who need not (in one or two instances who *may* not) be a member of the compact agency. By and large the chairmanship of compact agencies rotates frequently, to give each state a chance in the chair; and the position is not one of great power. In a few cases, one person has remained in the chair long enough to make an impression on the work of the agency, as did Howard S. Cullmann of the Port of New York Authority. No compact specifies the duties of the officers, these being

[36] An exception to the rule is the Upper Colorado River Compact, which declares that the United States representative shall merely be "entitled to the same powers and rights as the Commissioners" of the party states. Article VIII, a.

left to the agency itself to settle in its by-laws. In assigning their duties, the compact bodies ordinarily follow the usual pattern for such officers.

In addition to specifying some of the officers to be chosen, compacts usually go into considerable detail with regard to mechanics, especially in connection with the meetings of the bodies they set up. Meetings are required to be held at least once, and, in a number of compacts, twice a year. Often, the compact expressly permits the commission to meet at any place within the compacting states, but even where the permission is absent, the power is accepted as being inherent in compact agencies. It is generally felt that rotating meeting places enables the compact officers to see for themselves the problems in their areas of concern better than they would be able to do if they met always in the same place. The Gulf States Marine Fisheries Commission's "plan of rotating meetings from state to state assists the body to gain knowledge of fisheries problems in all areas," comments the Secretary-Treasurer of that group,[37] and virtually the same comments have been made about most of the other commissions which include three or more states. It is of course also politically expedient to change meeting places in order not to seem to show preference for one party state over another.

In all cases, the requirements of a quorum are set down together with a provision for method of voting. Thus the framework within which a compact agency may work as it sets out to exercise its powers has to a large extent already been determined for it by the framers of the com-

[37] W. Dudley Gunn to Richard H. Leach, February 10, 1956.

pact, and this despite the fact that in almost every case the compact creates the agency as a permanent body politic and endows it with all the powers usually belonging to such bodies. These include, in addition to the powers just described, the power to adopt and use an official seal; to adopt suitable by-laws and regulations for the conduct of business; to appoint committees; to establish and maintain an office or offices; to employ a staff; to enter into contracts; to sue and be sued; to acquire real and personal property; and to hold, sell, rent, or otherwise dispose of such property at its discretion. These powers make each compact agency a self-contained operating unit. Each is thus given a more independent position than ordinary state agencies, but it is more a matter of appearance than of fact. For, as noted above, the states are careful to keep a number of strings attached to compact agencies; and, though they do not often pull them, the possibility exists that they might do so at any time. Even so, the freedom a compact agency may exercise in the selection of its own officers, in the adoption of its own rules of procedure (within the broad limits set down in the compact), and in the employment of staff serve to set it aside from other state agencies; and it may account in part for the difficulty states have had in integrating compact agencies into their administrative framework.

The power to adopt by-laws is especially significant because it permits the compact agency to develop the details of its own operation in the way which suits it best. Because by-laws may be changed easily, the methodology of day-to-day business can be accommodated to actual needs and situations. The Atlantic States Marine Fisheries Compact, for example, contemplated that the Commission would function as a single unit and made no provision for the very different fishery interests of its several member states. Before the Commission had been at work long, it discovered that the entire Commission could not work as a unit "because the southerners were bored when the northerners were discussing lobsters and the northerners got restless when the southerners were discussing shrimp and croaker." [38] The utility of the Commission was saved by making a provision in the by-laws "for the more effective integration" of its work: the Commission was divided into four Sections, each dealing with a recognized unit of the coast with common fisheries problems.[39] The Sections have worked out well, and there is little doubt that the Commission's work has been greatly facilitated by them.

Because of the power to adopt their own by-laws, compact agencies are not encased in the strait-jackets in which many of their sister agencies in the states find themselves. Although of course they remain subject to the power of the parent state legislatures, just as their sister agencies do, that power is seldom exercised after the agency is launched. Thus they may use their power to enact by-laws to reorient themselves as experience requires and set their own course, limited only by the broad

[38] Wayne D. Heydecker, Secretary-Treasurer, Atlantic States Marine Fisheries Commission, to Richard H. Leach, July 15, 1954.

[39] Rules and Regulations, Atlantic States Marine Fisheries Commission, Article II, section 2.

purposes of the compacts. Where the compact, by design or indirection, permits alternate courses, the by-laws become even more important. The Southern Regional Education Compact, for example, was drawn up with the conviction, which the ratifying state legislatures evidently shared, that the chief concern of the Southern Regional Education Board ought to be "the development, establishment, acquisition, operation, and maintenance" of regional schools and institutions of higher education. Early experience demonstrated to the Board that such an orientation simply was not feasible. When the by-laws of the Board were adopted in 1949, they declared: "In so far as possible, needed regional educational services shall be provided through special arrangements among existing institutions." Facilities operated by the Board, the by-laws went on, were to be resorted to only when no existing institution in the region, either alone or in cooperation with others, could supply satisfactory services.[40] Thus the main purpose of the Board, as originally conceived, was changed by the Board after the Compact became effective, with the result that the by-laws have assumed really as great importance in subsequent Board activities as the Compact itself.

By-laws are not the only avenue open to those who seek to change the direction of a compact agency. Most compacts contain a provision like that in the Palisades Interstate Park Compact which states that the "commission shall also have such additional functions, jurisdiction, rights, powers and duties as may be conferred

[40] By-Laws, Southern Regional Education Board, Article I, sec. 3, d.

upon it by both states." [41] Even if such a provision is lacking, it is obvious that, as tools of the states, all compact agencies may be utilized as the several party states see fit. An extensive alteration might necessitate resubmission of the compact to Congress for its approval, but that too is perfectly possible to do. The Interstate Sanitation Compact was originally confined to the study of water pollution, but New York and New Jersey have empowered it to study air pollution with the consent but without the participation of the third party, Connecticut. If recent recommendations are followed, the Interstate Commission on the Potomac River Basin, which has thus far been concerned solely with pollution abatement, may be given a broader scope by the states to permit it to "expand its field of interest into the general resources and conservation fields as they relate to water." [42] Given a sincere desire by the states to make use of a compact agency—i.e., to recognize it as a power unit—there is no barrier to their making and remaking it as circumstances dictate.

Generally speaking, three kinds of power are delegated to compact agencies. A few are endowed with operating powers, or, as the Palisades Park Compact puts it, are designed to perform "governmental functions of the [party] states. . . ." [43] Where this is the case, the states have not been niggardly in their delegation of authority, perhaps because in nearly every case each state had already tried

[41] Palisades Interstate Park Compact, Article III.
[42] Interstate Commission for the Potomac River Basin, *News-Letter*, XIII (September, 1957).
[43] Palisades Interstate Park Compact, Article II.

to solve the particular problem or set of problems single-handedly, had failed, and thus had concluded that the delegation of its own powers to a compact agency could only result in their more effective application. The Waterfront Commission of New York Harbor, for example, was created by New York and New Jersey out of a desperate need felt by both states to eliminate criminal and corrupt practices in the handling of waterborne freight within the Port of New York and to regularize conditions of employment of waterfront labor. Neither state had been able to root out the traditional pier practices of the "shape-up" and public loading, or to put an end to the violent and unauthorized labor disturbances that had long characterized the port area. With the creation of the Waterfront Commission, both states delegated enough of their own powers to enable the Commission to control waterfront evils.

To the Palisades Interstate Park Commission were transferred "all of the functions, jurisdiction, rights, powers and duties of the respective state [Palisades Park] boards . . ." [44] It, too, was created after long experience with separate state boards had demonstrated the need for a joint interstate agency to meet the recreation and conservation needs of the area. When the decision was made in 1937 to create the Commission, the states handed over their powers to it intact.

The Port of New York Authority and the Delaware River Port Authority were likewise created because the party states had found that the exercise of their own powers independently of the other states was inadequate

[44] Palisades Interstate Park Compact, Article III.

and ineffective. In both cases, the party states delegated power generously to the Compact agency. As the General Counsel for the Port of New York Authority remarked recently, the achievements of that Authority "have been possible only because its founding fathers had the foresight to arm it with broad general powers commensurate with its functions and purposes. . . ." [45] Although the Delaware Port Authority has not been directed to engage in so comprehensive a program, the Compact leaves no doubt that the party states intended it to be as effective as the Port of New York Authority. The states have tended to delegate additional powers to both authorities rather than to restrict or withdraw them.

The generosity with which powers have been granted to such agencies may be seen in more detail by glancing at the provisions of the Compact establishing the Delaware River Port Authority. In addition to the usually delegated powers over internal operation and organization, discussed above, the Port Authority is given power to

borrow money upon its bonds or other obligations and to make such agreements as it deems necessary with the holders of such bonds as to the management and operation of any property or facility owned or controlled by it, the tolls, rents, rates or other charges to be . . . collected [by it] . . . or the application . . . of the proceeds [from] any bonds or other obligations. . . .

[45] Address of Sidney Goldstein before the Section on Municipal Law of the American Bar Association, London, England, July 25, 1957 (Mimeographed release), 2.

exercise the right of eminent domain within the Port District.

acquire, purchase, construct, lease, operate, maintain and undertake any project, including any terminal, terminal facility, transportation facility, or any other facility of commerce and to make charges for the use thereof.

determine the exact location, system and character of and all other matters in connection with any and all of the improvements or facilities which it may be authorized to own, construct, establish, effectuate, operate or control.

make expenditures anywhere in the United States and foreign countries, to pay commissions, and hire or contract with experts and consultants, and otherwise to do indirectly anything which the Commission may do directly.

exercise all other powers not inconsistent with the constitutions of the two States or of the United States, which may be reasonably necessary or incidental to the effectuation of its authorized purposes or to the exercise of any of the foregoing powers, except the power to levy taxes or assessments, and generally to exercise in connection with its property and affairs . . . any and all powers which might be exercised by a natural person or a private corporation in connection with similar property and affairs.[46]

There can hardly be any doubt that the party states

[46] Delaware River Port Authority Compact, Article IV, i-l, n-p.

meant to create an agency with considerable power to act for them. If controls were also placed in the Compact— and a great many were—they were inserted to provide against the abuses of such power rather than to limit its exercise.

The powers vested in the study-recommendatory commissions are not nearly so broad. In the first place, there is seldom the virtually complete delegation by the party states of their powers in the fields in which the interstate agencies operate. Usually, the party states give the compact agency a part and permit existing state agencies to retain the rest without clearly determining mutual relations. The Atlantic and Gulf Marine Fisheries Commissions, for example, although given by their Compacts the duty of ascertaining "from time to time such methods, practices, circumstances and conditions as may be disclosed for bringing about the conservation and the prevention of the depletion and physical waste of the fisheries" of their respective sea coasts, are not the only agencies so directed by the party states. Each state maintains its own separate agency or agencies operating at least partially in the same field of inquiry and directed to make their own recommendations to the legislature. Indeed, both Compacts require that one member of each Commission be an officer of such an agency. In the second place, the study agencies are not always given sufficient power to make their studies themselves. The Atlantic and Gulf Marine Fisheries Commissions, to use them as an example again, are bound by their Compacts to use the U.S. Fish and Wildlife Service to perform their research. Other compact agencies are similarly required to work through existing state or federal agencies doing research in their particular fields of interest. Thus for many study agencies, the chief function is really coordination and not study at all. In the words of the long-time Secretary-Treasurer of the Atlantic Marine Fisheries Commission: "You may find it desirable to consider the possibility that the establishment of an interstate research agency might in itself be undesirable if the work involved duplicating work normally within the sphere of either the state or federal research agencies. We so conceived it, therefore our Commission was designed primarily as an instrument for coordination of effort along the Atlantic coast." [47]

Other compact agencies find themselves in the same situation. The Western Interstate Commission for Higher Education states frankly that it "has no program of its own to impose. [Its] role is that of a catalyst . . . [It] *is simply a vehicle for those states and those institutions willing to search for new ways of working together.*" [48] Even though Article I of the Compact declares that the Commission's goal is the cooperative provision of "acceptable and efficient educational facilities to meet the needs of the Region and of the students thereof," it does not grant to the Commission power to provide those facilities. The party states retain that power and endow the Commission only with the lesser power to try to persuade the several states to "join to-

[47] Wayne D. Heydecker to Richard H. Leach, July 15, 1954.
[48] *Working Together in the West through WICHE, Annual Report,* Western Interstate Commission for Higher Education (1955), 6.

gether in working out overall, long-range solutions to problems common to all." [49]

Similarly, although the Interstate Oil Compact was written out of a concern to prevent waste of the nation's oil resources, and although it imposes on the Interstate Oil Compact Commission the duty of studying "methods, practices, circumstances, and conditions . . . for bringing about conservation and the prevention of physical waste of oil and gas," it does not give the Commission power to impose a general pattern of conservation, based on its findings, on the states. The Commission has no power of compulsion or coercion whatsoever; it can only affect state conservation laws by the logic of its arguments.

Even though two water pollution compact agencies are endowed with power to compel compliance with the standards they set, they have used it in a relatively small number of instances. Both the Ohio River Valley Water Sanitation Commission and the Interstate Sanitation Commission have chosen instead to rely on persuasion and public education. Though both Compacts grant power to use state courts to enforce the Commissions' requirements, both Commissions have "put their badges in their pockets" and have depended upon the compulsion of facts. And that policy has been successful. "During the twenty-year life of the [Interstate Sanitation] Commission 58 municipalities have built or improved

[49] *From Idea to Reality: The Progress and Potentials of the Western Interstate Commission for Higher Education* (1954), 11.

sewage plants without compulsion. In only 10 cases was court action necessary." [50] The Ohio Commission's educational efforts have also succeeded. On the basis of this record, when the Interstate Commission on the Potomac River Basin's Compact Study Committee reviewed the powers given that Commission—which do not include the power of enforcement—it concluded that "except for the moral effect of interstate action against a polluter, very little of real value would come out of investing Ohio-type compact power in the Potomac Commission." [51]

Persuasion is also an essential tool of the other types of interstate compact agency. The operating agencies are charged with recommending action they may deem desirable to the legislatures of the party states; and, in securing favorable action, they are in the same position as the purely recommendatory agencies. The Port of New York Authority uses persuasion as much as the Interstate Oil Compact Commission or the Western Interstate Commission for Higher Education.[52] The executive officers of the Port Authority appear before legislatures and governors, and the general public as well, as often as members of the staff of any recommendatory agency to plead its case. Both types of agency must depend heavily on their ability to convince legislative and administrative bodies that their recommendations should be adopted. Public relations work has therefore assumed

[50] *Cleaning Up the Doorway to America*, 4.
[51] Interstate Commission on the Potomac River Basin, *News Letter*, XIII (September, 1957).
[52] See Bard, *The Port of New York Authority*, 105–39.

as much importance in compact agencies as it has in other segments of our national life.

The real nature of their power may be brought home more forcefully when the powers actually vested in one or two recommendatory compact agencies are brought under close scrutiny. The New England Higher Education Compact gives the New England Board of Higher Education power to "(1) collect, correlate, and evaluate data in the fields of its interest under the compact; to publish reports, bulletins, and other documents making available the results of its research; and, in its discretion, to charge fees for said reports, bulletins and documents; (2) enter into such contractual agreements or arrangements with any of the compacting states or agencies thereof and with educational institutions and agencies as may be required in the judgment of the board to provide adequate services and facilities in educational fields covered by this compact . . ."; and to make such recommendations for legislative action by the party states as it deems advisable in relation to both these powers.[53] The utility of the whole enterprise obviously depends much more on how effective the Board is in persuading someone to act on its findings than in merely producing new sets of statistics and new articles on methodology. Just as obviously, no state or institution will enter into a contract to provide educational services for the region until it has been convinced of the wisdom and necessity of doing so. The Board must therefore promote contracts if it wishes them to be used at all.

[53] New England Higher Education Compact, Article V.

The Interstate Commission on the Potomac River Basin is authorized as follows:

1. To coordinate, tabulate, and summarize existing data on the pollution, character, and condition of the streams of the [basin].
2. To supplement existing data, if necessary, by conducting investigations.
3. To promote adoption by the signatory bodies of uniform legislation for the control of stream pollution.
4. To disseminate information to the public on the effects of stream pollution and the objectives of the commission.
5. To cooperate with other organizations in, and conduct, if advisable, studies of treatment methods for sewage and industrial wastes.
6. To recommend to the signatory bodies standards for cleanliness of streams.[54]

Again, the Compact suggests the necessity of promotion and persuasion. The Commission has always acted on that suggestion. Summarizing its work over 15 years, the Commission recently noted that it has devoted "the major share of its . . . efforts towards diagnosing the ills of the Potomac and acquainting the public with the results of the diagnosis. The framers of the Compact . . . were of the opinion that no anti-pollution legislation or ordinances . . . will be truly effective unless the public at large understands the problems involved, and

[54] Interstate Compact for the Potomac River Basin, Article II.

accepts the desired goals as reasonable and desirable ends." [55] To provide that understanding and make possible that acceptance has been the Commission's concern since its founding in 1940.

The third type of interstate agency is represented by the seven water apportionment commissions, which administer the technical details involved in the equitable allocation of certain waters to the party states. Though all these commissions have an incidental recommendatory power, and one or two of them additional developmental powers,[56] their primary concern remains to supervise the adherence of the states to the limits set by the various compacts to the amount of water each may store or divert, and to authorize exceptions thereto. Their most characteristic activity is the operation of stream gaging stations, from which they secure the data from which to judge adherence or violation. The water agencies are given no power to act against a violating state and may only point out the fact to appropriate state offi-

[55] Interstate Commission on the Potomac River Basin, *News Letter*, XI (June, 1955).

[56] The Upper Colorado River Compact, for example, gives the Commission the power to "secure expeditious agricultural and industrial development in the Upper Basin" and to protect life and property from floods (Article I), and under this grant, the Commission has been active in collecting data and preparing legislation for the Colorado River Storage Project for presentation to Congress. The Pecos River Compact likewise provides for the development of the water resources in the river basin, and the Pecos River Commission has undertaken an ambitious Water Salvage and Salinity Alleviation Program. It, too, seeks to enlist the aid of the federal government in bringing the desired end about.

cials. Remedial action, if any be taken, must be initiated by the states themselves. The Arkansas River Compact is typical in this regard:

Violation of any of the provisions of this Compact or other actions prejudicial thereto which come to the attention of the [Arkansas River] Administration shall be promptly investigated by it. When deemed advisable as a result of such investigation, the Administration may report its findings and recommendations to the State official who is charged with the administration of water rights for appropriate action, it being the intent of this Compact that enforcement of its terms shall be accomplished in general through State agencies and officials . . . .[57]

The water commissions, of course, are not by themselves in lacking enforcement power. Generally, this vital power is left in the hands of the party states. Even the Port of New York Authority is denied it. "The two states," reads Article XIX of the Compact, "shall provide penalties for violations of any order, rule or regulation of the Port Authority, and for the manner of enforcing same." Even where a limited power of enforcement is given a compact agency, it has been found expedient not to use it. In this particular, compact agencies differ markedly from their sister agencies in the states: to the latter is generally confided the power of enforcement; to the former chiefly the power of persuasion.

The roles of the compact agencies do not vary a great

[57] Arkansas River Compact, Article VIII, H.

deal, despite the kind of power entrusted to them. The operating agencies have the most active role to play and the water commissions the least, but all of them tend to operate more as policy-makers than as executives. For most, their role is very like that of a board of directors, one of review and not of origination. Their function is confined largely to discussing alternative courses of action to implement the objectives of the compacts under which they operate. The alternative courses, however, are for the most part suggested to them by committees or staff. If the agencies are able, they hire staff to execute policy. The agency as a whole usually only selects an executive director (usually upon the recommendation of the executive committee), who then exercises for the agency the rest of the hiring power. Of course the agency may formulate and adopt regulations within which the staff must work and to some extent coordinate and supervise staff operations.

Whatever type of power is exercised by a compact agency, meetings of its appointed members are mandatory under the terms of every compact. Most of the agencies meet more often than the once a year usually required, the water apportionment and study commissions meeting less frequently than the operating agencies. The latter meet as often as business necessitates, even several times a month on occasion. The former usually have a regular so-called annual meeting and one or two other meetings in addition. The Interstate Oil Compact Commission used to have quarterly meetings but recently changed to two meetings a year. The Ohio River Valley Water Sanitation Commission meets quarterly still, as do one or two other agencies. Generally, however, the compact bodies meet two or three times a year. Meetings vary from the convention-type public meetings of the Interstate Oil Compact Commission to the strictly parliamentary meetings of the Sabine River Compact Administration to the meetings of the Interstate Sanitation Commission, which to some seem to "have the quality of a Quaker meeting." [58]

A typical Interstate Oil Compact Commission semiannual meeting draws 500 to 600 people and runs over two days, the first being devoted to committee meetings (also open to the public) and the second to a general session. The latter follows the usual convention pattern: roll call, an address of welcome, a response to the welcoming address, the chairman's address, introductions, the main address (usually on a technical subject), committee reports, reports of advisory committees, an open forum, and adjournment. Business matters are taken up at a special business meeting. Care is taken to arrange the meetings at a succession of attractive resorts or in a different city each time, where social amenities may be observed along with business.

If no other compact agency makes quite the production out of its meetings that the IOCC does, a number of the larger ones hold meetings in much the same pattern. The Western Interstate Commission for Higher Education, the Atlantic States Marine Fisheries Commission, the Southern Regional Education Board, and the New England Interstate Water Pollution Control Commission are all too big to permit informal, unstructured,

[58] *Cleaning Up the Doorway to America,* 5.

give-and-take meetings of the whole. Besides, the purpose of these agencies, like that of the Interstate Oil Compact Commission, is to a large extent to interest and involve the public in their activities, and convention-type meetings are well suited to that purpose.

The operating agencies tend to be strictly business-like at their meetings, since the initiation and conduct of operating programs depend on decisions made there. The Port of New York Authority usually meets once a month to consider an agenda prepared by its staff, a copy of which has already been sent to each member for his study and consideration. Meetings are usually held in the late afternoon of a week-day in the Port Authority's offices at 111 Eighth Avenue in downtown New York. They seldom last more than two hours. They are open to the public (except when the Authority resolves itself into the committee of the whole), but neither the time of day nor the procedure encourages public attendance. The agenda is usually followed carefully. Appropriate members of the staff are present to answer questions, but extensive debate and discussion seldom take place. Resolutions have been prepared in advance by the staff department concerned and are almost always passed unanimously. Essential business is thus dispatched with a maximum of efficiency, and the social role which convention-type meetings fill is ignored altogether. Members usually live in the same general area, and their meetings do not involve any special departure from their routine.

The water apportionment commissions, because their compacts so restrict the scope of their activities, conduct generally routine annual meetings. The by-laws of the

Sabine River Compact Administration provide that the order of business at each meeting shall consist of the following: call to order, reading of the minutes of the last meeting, approval of those minutes, report of the chairman, report of the secretary, report of the treasurer, report of committees, unfinished business, new business, and adjournment.[59] In general, this pattern is adhered to strictly. There is ordinarily little new business to conduct, the chief purpose of the Administration being, like that of all the water commissions, to review water being used under the terms of the Compact and to determine if adjustments need to be made for the coming year. The Yellowstone River Compact Commission's rules and regulations declare that the primary purpose of its annual meeting is the "consideration of the annual report for the water year ending the preceding September 30th."[60] Some discussion takes place, of course, at its meetings, and at those of the other water commissions, but since all of them are concerned in the main with the preservation of an existing statutory situation and with exceptions thereto rather than with the development of a new pattern for the river basin concerned, their official actions are necessarily restricted.[61] The Upper Colorado Commission and the Pecos River Commission are the

[59] By-Laws of the Sabine River Compact Administration, Article IV, 8.

[60] Rules and Regulations for Administration of the Yellowstone River Compact, Article V.

[61] See Richard H. Leach, "The Interstate Compact, Water, and the Southwest: A Case Study in Compact Utility," *The Southwestern Social Science Quarterly*, XXXVIII (December, 1957), 236–47.

only ones which have utilized much meeting time in discussing matters other than those closely related to the apportionment provisions of the Compacts.

It should be noted that even the most limited type of compact commission meeting offers state and federal officers, as well as persons from related private agencies and organizations, an opportunity to discuss their common interests, to suggest programs and projects, to plan informal cooperation between their work and that of the compact commission concerned, and to express opinions as to the effectiveness with which compact objectives are being met. This type of contact, which also of course takes place in other situations throughout the year, is an invaluable side-effect of the meetings and should be recognized as one of their contributions to the solution of problems in their respective fields.

Regardless of their programs and the nature of their meetings, most compact agencies find it necessary to function through committees. Only the Canadian River Commission, the Yellowstone River Compact Commission, the Breaks Interstate Park Commission, the Lake Champlain Bridge Commission, and the Waterfront Commission of New York Harbor do not report the use of any committees. A two-man commission, the latter has from the beginning utilized staff rather than committees to perform the functions assigned to it by the Compact. Elsewhere the use of committees is commonplace. Even most of the smaller compact bodies find that committees assure better preparation and investigation of the subjects to be acted upon than could be obtained by the members; and the larger bodies are forced to divide the work among committees in order to get it done at all. The Southern Regional Education Board at full strength, for example, has 80 members; the Atlantic Marine Fisheries Commission, 45; the Western Interstate Commission for Higher Education, 33; the New England Interstate Water Pollution Control Commission, 35; and the Ohio River Valley Water Sanitation Commission, 27. Such groups can function only through committees. Moreover, committees operate informally, may function throughout the year, and may either employ experts in their subject-matter fields or be comprised of experts themselves. Most compacts and the by-laws of the agencies they establish do not require subject-matter committee members to be members of the compact bodies themselves. Thus proposals submitted to committees may be considered in greater detail and with greater care than would be possible if left to the commissions as a whole. Committees probably go far also to involve commission members in the work carried out under the compact and thus both heighten their interest and increase their feeling of responsibility.

The compact agencies employ both official committees, composed of their own members, which formulate policy or supervise its execution, and advisory committees made up of qualified consultants. The members of the former usually include representatives from each signatory state. The members of the latter, who sometimes include officials or staff members of the agencies, are more often than not outsiders who are appointed because of their special skills or knowledge. Neither type of committee member receives compensation for his services, though expenses are always absorbed by the compact agencies.

The most common committee of a compact agency is the executive committee, which typically exercises all the powers of the whole body during the intervals between its meetings. Like all such committees, the executive committees of most compact agencies act as pilots. They develop recommendations on policy and procedure which are usually accepted. In conjunction with the finance committee, the second most common type used by compact agencies, the executive committee largely determines the direction and emphasis of work under the compact.

The function of finance committees is usually broadly defined. The By-Laws of the Delaware River Port Authority state it as follows: "The Finance Committee shall consider and make recommendations upon all questions relating to the financing of any undertaking of the Authority and all questions relating to depositories of the Authority shall be referred to it and it shall consider and make recommendations upon any other matters dealing with finance that the Authority may, from time to time, refer to it." [62] The finance committee, or its equivalent, the budget committee, is as concerned with planning the spending of income as it is with raising it. Because the agency as a whole usually follows its recommendations on financial and budgetary matters, its importance is obvious.

Other common and important committees of compact agencies are the legal committee (for those which do not

[62] By-Laws, Delaware River Port Authority, Article VIII, B.

employ regular counsel), the by-laws committee (which influences internal operation), and the audit committee.

Perhaps even more important than their own committees to the study and water agencies, in particular, are subject-matter advisory committees. They often serve as executive staff, performing research and program development functions. In some cases this arrangement is necessary because financial restrictions make the employment of staff impossible. In other cases, it is deliberately chosen. The Western Interstate Commission for Higher Education, for example, declares that its programs "cannot emerge from the minds of a central staff. Educational and professional leaders in the states must always be the primary source of ideas. Ideas emerge only as responsible leaders participate in the work of the Commission—as consultants, advisers, and members of study groups." [63]

The water allocation commissions tend to rely heavily on engineering committees on which the officials responsible for water supply in each state usually serve. Their reports and recommendations are central to the successful execution of the compacts. The Sabine River Compact Administration's master basin map was prepared for it by its Engineering Advisory Committee; the Engineering Advisory Committee to the Pecos River Commission provides the data on which recommendations to the states and federal government for increased storage and irrigation facilities may be based and on which enforcement of the terms of the Compact depend; and the Engineer Advisors to the Rio Grande Compact

[63] *Working Together in the West* . . . , *loc. cit.*

Commission annually study the figures the party states report on their deliveries and determine whether to debit or credit each state under the terms of the Compact.

The study agencies generally make use of a wider variety of committees, some of them permanent standing committees, others created on an *ad hoc* basis, each of which studies its field of interest and reports at annual or special meetings of the agencies and often by publication to a broader audience as well. The members of such committees are usually experts and leaders in each state in the committee's particular area of concern. They may be scientists, lawyers, engineers, dentists, geologists, deans of graduate schools or engineering colleges, teachers, industrialists, or state and local governmental officials, depending on the nature of the committee's assignment. Very seldom does a study commission or board act without having heard a committee's recommendation. What has been said of the Interstate Oil Compact Commission applies in some degree to all of the study commissions: "The basic contributions of the . . . Commission are not made in general meetings . . . but rather in the regular and special meetings of [the] committees. . . ." [64] The Oil Compact Commission always freely acknowledges its debt to the "earnest and qualified men who give unstintingly of their time and their knowledge in this important work." [65]

[64] Remarks of Governor Allan Shivers to the 1951 Winter Meeting of the Interstate Oil Compact Commission. *The Interstate Oil Compact Quarterly Bulletin*, X (December, 1951), 18.
[65] *Ibid.* Similar remarks are made several times at every meeting of the IOCC.

The use the Interstate Oil Compact Commission has made of subject-matter committees is illustrative of the reliance the study commissions, in general, have come to place on such committees. The IOCC presently relies on six standing committees, which perform the core of the Commission's work:

(1) *The Engineering Committee studies and reports on production methods and principles, studies engineering problems, and recommends ways and means of increasing ultimate recovery of gas and oil. Topics for study and discussion are solicited from members of the Committee, from state conservation agencies, and from representatives of the oil and state conservation agencies, and from representatives of the oil and gas industries. Among other projects, the Committee has recently completed a book on oil and gas production, studied the engineering problems encountered in the underground storage of gas, and explored the possibility of increased ultimate recovery of oil by the utilization of natural gas in the production process.*

(2) *The Legal Committee studies the complex legal aspects of conservation, prepares model conservation statutes for use by the states, and reports on current court cases and legal developments affecting conservation laws in the several states. The Committee also keeps a current summary of all state conservation laws and publishes, in cooperation with the Mineral Section of the American*

Bar Association, an annual report on conservation activities in the several states.

(3) The Public Lands Committee studies and reports on the problems encountered in oil and gas production on federal and state-owned lands. The long-time chairman of the Committee once stated its purpose as "to be alert to oppose legislation inimical to the best interests of the Public Land States."

(4) The Regulatory Practices Committee prepares model sets of rules and regulations for the conservation of oil and gas for use by state regulatory agencies and suggests uniform forms for reporting purposes.

(5) The Secondary Recovery and Pressure Maintenance Committee studies and reports on methods for increasing oil recovery and encourages research in secondary recovery and pressure maintenance. The Director of the Technical Services Division of IOCC is especially concerned with secondary recovery problems. With his assistance, state secondary recovery committees have been established in a number of states. In cooperation with the Commission, these state committees have published a number of technical bulletins in the last few years.

(6) The Research Committee assembles and disseminates data on such things as the demand for oil, conservation laws and practices in the several states, and results achieved by different conservation methods. Special projects are often con-

ducted, such as a recent one on the problem of well spacing and its controlling factors.[66]

In addition to these standing committees, special committees are often appointed to advise the Commission on particular problems. Thus, an Imports Committee was created in 1957 to study the effect of oil imports on state oil conservation programs.

The Southern Regional Education Board has also made extensive use of committees, advisory councils, and commissions. A study group is usually created as the first step in the Board's approach to any new program activity. Its recommendations normally are decisive as to whether the Board will establish the program. If a program is recommended and subsequently established, a permanent committee, composed of representatives of the institutions involved and the Board, is appointed to oversee it. A member of the Board staff usually works with the committee as secretary. The several committees are autonomous within the confines of their programs. In addition, the Board makes use of "regional councils," composed of representatives of industry, government and professional associations, to work with the regional committees in planning for training and research in such various fields as mental health, forestry, and psychology.

The Interstate Commission for the Potomac River Basin, wishing to "work in close harmony with the poli-

[66] On (3) above, see W. M. Downing's speech to the 1954 Meeting of the Interstate Oil Compact Commission, *The Interstate Oil Compact Quarterly Bulletin*, XIII (December, 1954), 38.

cies of the various state agencies and industrial establishments" in the Basin and to obtain "technical advice from them," [67] appointed two advisory committees in the early days of its operation: a Technical Committee and an Industrial Committee. The former consists of the directors of state planning boards and state sanitary engineers and their federal equivalents; the latter of representatives of industry within the Basin. Since then, a Recreation and Wildlife Committee, a Land Committee, and a Water Committee have also been established.

On the whole, the appointed members of compact bodies seem to take both their duties in connection with the agency as a whole and those in connection with the committees to which they may belong quite seriously. Except for the members of the Port of New York Authority and the Delaware River Port Authority, who may spend from fifty to sixty days a year on Authority business, and the members of the Waterfront Commission of New York Harbor, who work almost full time, the average commissioner spends from ten to fifteen days a year on commission business. It appears that compact officials devote time to their duties chiefly out of interest and public spirit. Most commissioners are, in the words of one of them, "independent, interested and responsible citizens," and this feeling accounts probably for much of their attention to their jobs. Perhaps because they are in a sense pioneers in government, they feel an additional keenness about their jobs.

The attitude of interstate compact officials is exemplified by the work of Arthur C. King, a member of the

[67] *Fifth Annual Report* (1946), 3.

Delaware River Port Authority and its predecessors. On the occasion of his death, the Authority declared:

His record of faithful service was extraordinary. He had not been absent from any meeting of the Authority or its predecessor commissions or of any committee of which he was a member for more than 28 years. . . . Despite failing health, he took a deep interest in the construction of the Walt Whitman Bridge, served as chairman of the special committee which acted upon acquisition of property for the structure. . . . At the time of his death, he was chairman of the Committee on Insurance and Pensions, and an active member of the Executive, Finance, and Transportation Committees.[68]

Despite their interest in the work of the agencies to which they belong, it is probable, however, that few commissioners have any general or theoretical interest in compact agencies as such. Many of them come to their jobs with a fairly narrow concept of interstate compacts and their potential uses; and, once at work, they have little occasion to see what they are doing as it fits into a broader context. They are inclined to see the practical job to be done and not to be concerned with where it fits into political theory. Only one of the respondents to the questionnaire circulated by the authors, for example, even attempted, as the questionnaire asked, to "comment frankly on his conception of . . . interstate agencies and their place in the federal system."

[68] *Report of the Delaware River Port Authority of Pennsylvania and New Jersey* (1957), 27.

Most of the respondents used this space to describe the kinds of functions preformed by the compact agency of which they were members. Two commented that they did not understand what was meant by the request.

The one commissioner who did respond wrote that he viewed "these regional commissions as confederacies operating within a union." "We are banded together," he went on, "for mutual support and common action. We can join or secede, but our very existence as a group acknowledges the need for group action in certain [areas], but not [for] total, national action." But if he seems to have thought about the place of interstate compact agencies in the American political context, he is the exception that proves the rule. For the great majority of compact commissioners regard themselves as men with the limited responsibility "to build confidence in the program and to effect a sensible balance between need for action, and ability to take action. . . ." [69] They shun conceptual thinking about their jobs and do not dream of new regional units of government or of making compacts a sort of third force in American government and politics. Most commissioners probably do not even have a very firm belief in regional planning. They regard their duties as an extension of state activities and themselves as state officials who happen to be working on programs in cooperation with counterparts in sister states.

Although the boards and commissions established by interstate compact are legally constituted action agencies, many of them operate, as has been indicated, through committees and staffs. The appointed members of the

[69] *Cleaning Up the Doorway to America,* 4.

compact agencies are not usually able to devote enough time to their programs to assure success, or even to devise policy; and so it comes about that many commissions are, in effect, legislative bodies dependent upon executive personnel. The staffs of most of the compact agencies have assumed coordinate roles in attaining the goals of the compacts. Thus an analysis of staff is as important as the examination of the commissions and boards in understanding the administration of interstate compacts.

4: Interstate Compact Agencies:

Staffing and Operations

The commissions and boards established by interstate compact, although legally responsible agents of the compacting states, generally count on their staffs not only for the execution of policy but also for major assistance in its formulation. All the members of compact agencies carry on their functions along with other regular occupations. Although they are able to formulate policy and establish general program direction, adopt and promulgate rules and regulations, and even in some cases to work for the program's accomplishment through public relations or some other form of personal involvement, they are unable to handle the day-to-day problems and the details of policy execution which arise even under the most limited compacts. Thus in order for the expectations of the framers of the compacts to be realized, staff assistance of one kind or another is necessary for most of the compact agencies. "The staff," notes a publication of the Ohio

113

River Valley Water Sanitation Commission, "is the administrative arm of the Commission. It executes the program. It conducts the detailed studies and makes recommendations on the basis of which the Commission can decide policy questions. Operation of all financial, legal and other administrative functions is the responsibility of the staff." [1]

As partners, then, commission and staff achieve the ends of most of the compacts. A few programs require a large and varied staff; most require only the services of a few specialists in relatively narrow fields. Some compact programs have been developed to operate public facilities; the employees of the commissions in such cases are chiefly operating personnel. The majority of the agencies are designed primarily to serve the party states in a planning and coordinating capacity; the employees of these agencies perform mainly research and advisory functions. Whatever the case, long-range success of most interstate compacts depends quite as much upon the ability and effort of the staff as it does upon the members of the board or commission.

Fortunately, the framers of all but two of the compacts now in operation in the United States recognized the need for staff assistance and provided for it in the compacts. Thus the same paragraph of the Ohio River Valley Water Sanitation Compact that deals with the organization of the Commission declares that the Commission *"shall* appoint, and at its pleasure remove or dis-

[1] "What We Are Doing and How It Is Being Done," (a worksheet of the Ohio River Valley Water Sanitation Commission, 1950), 1.

charge, such officers and legal, clerical, expert and other assistants as may be required to carry the provisions of this Compact into effect. . . ." [2] While other compacts merely provide that the commission "*may* appoint and remove or discharge such officers and . . . assistants and employees as may be required . . . ," [3] the very fact that the power is singled out suggests that the framers of the compacts intended it to be used. For like all bodies corporate and politic, compact agencies presumably have the inherent power to hire and fire within the limits of the funds made available to them for that purpose. Thus both the Interstate Oil Compact Commission and the Southern Regional Education Board, neither of which is granted by its compact the right to employ staff, have done so from the beginning without the slightest legal difficulty and with no objection from the party states. The most stringent limitation on the use of staff appears in the Rio Grande Compact, which authorizes the Commission to employ only such staff as may be "reasonably necessary" to carry out the provisions of the Compact;[4] and that of course amounts to no restriction at all.

In addition, most compacts provide that the commissions shall be free from the necessity of observing the civil service regulations of the several participating states. The Interstate Compact on the Potomac River Basin, for example, specifically declares that staff "may be employed

[2] Ohio River Valley Water Sanitation Compact, Article V. Italics supplied.

[3] The wording of the Breaks Interstate Park Compact, Article IV. Italics supplied. This wording is common to almost every compact.

[4] Rio Grande Compact, Article XII.

without regard to any civil service or other similar requirements for employees" of any of the parties to the Compact.[5] Generally, the statement that the commission may appoint the employees it deems necessary, and "shall fix and determine their duties, qualifications and compensation, and may at its pleasure remove or discharge any such officer or employee," [6] which is included in a variety of wordings somewhere in most compacts, is considered to grant the necessary exemption. Every compact agency thus has an opportunity to develop the personnel arrangements which work best for it and is freed from the restrictions which otherwise might bind it to the patterns prevailing in the party states.

Consequently, there is no single pattern of compact staff arrangements. The use made of the power to employ staff differs from commission to commission. One or two agencies have so limited a program that little or no formal arrangement for staff need be made. The Canadian River Commission, for example, is charged by its Compact with two chief activities: supervising the adherence of the three party states to the water use rights established in the Compact and providing for the construction of additional works for the conservation of the waters of the Canadian River. For the former function, the Commission relies on information supplied by the states, and in the exercise of the latter it is confined to making recommendations to the states, who then undertake the actual construction of dams and reservoirs. Both

[5] Interstate Compact on the Potomac River Basin, Article I, B.
[6] The wording of the Northeastern Interstate Forest Fire Protection Compact, Article VII.

functions can only be performed by the Commission itself, and in neither activity has the Commission seemed
to need the services of staff. Before it acts, it does, of
course, receive a great deal of informal advice and information from others in the Compact area and elsewhere, and this, combined with the knowledge and experience of the Commissioners themselves, has so far
been adequate. A member of the Commission serves as
secretary and handles what little business there is to be
transacted between meetings and makes the necessary
preparations for each meeting, thus avoiding the necessity of going outside the Commission for even this type
of service.

The Canadian River Commission is the only compact
agency, however, which has not made any arrangements
for staff assistance at all. A number of the other water
commissions have provided for staff assistance and at the
same time avoided the necessity of hiring staffs of their
own either by calling on related agencies in the states and
federal government for assistance or by contracting with
the U.S. Geological Survey for the performance of whatever they need in the way of staff work. The Arkansas
River Compact Administration has worked so far chiefly
through state and federal agencies. Under the terms of
the Compact, Colorado and Kansas are bound to provide
the Administration with such assistance as it deems
necessary to carry out its apportionment duties and to
furnish upon request whatever factual data it requires. In
addition, the Compact "requests" the Director of the
U.S. Geological Survey and the Commissioner of Reclamation to collaborate with the Administration in the

execution of its duties. Under these directions, state officials and regional representatives of the two federal offices, as well as of the Corps of Engineers, have provided the Administration with all the data and information it has needed. Thus, though the Administration is permitted to supplement such assistance by hiring a staff of its own, it has not felt the need to do so, beyond the employment of an "administrative secretary-treasurer," whose duties are merely to order the gates of the John Martin Dam opened and closed to comply with the demands made for water from it by the two states under the terms of the Compact during the irrigating season, to keep the minutes of the quarterly meetings of the Administration, and to pay its bills.[7]

The Pecos River Commission, the Yellowstone River Compact Commission, the Sabine River Compact Administration, and the Rio Grande Compact Commission all take care of their staff problem through a yearly contract for engineering and clerical services with the U.S. Geological Survey. The Surface Water Offices of the U.S.G.S. collect a large part of the data needed for the administration of all four Compacts as part of their regular duties, and it seemed logical as well as less expensive to ask the Director of the Survey to permit a regular arrangement to be established whereby that data could be transmitted directly to the commissions and which would enable the commissions to be serviced by experts in water matters. The Director approved of the idea, and under the agreement concluded with the Survey, each commis-

[7] Hackett Smartt, Secretary, Arkansas River Compact Administration, to Richard H. Leach, April 4, 1958.

sion designates an engineer in a U.S.G.S. office near the river concerned to serve the commission as secretary. That person then assumes the role as a part of his regular federal job, and the commission pays the Survey for the time he devotes to commission work. The chairmen of the Rio Grande and Yellowstone Commissions are U.S.G.S. officials, and they combine their positions as chairmen with the job as secretary and handle all Commission business through their offices. In the case of the other two commissions, different persons serve as chairman and as secretary, and the Commission work is handled through the secretary's office.

In general, the contracts with U.S.G.S. follow the pattern of the agreement between the Rio Grande Compact Commission and U.S.G.S., which provides that the Survey shall:

(1) *Collect and correlate all factual data and other records having a material bearing on the administration of the Compact and keep each Commissioner advised thereof.*

(2) *Inspect all gaging stations required for administration of the Compact and make recommendations to the Commission as to any changes or improvements [which need to be made.]*

(3) *Report to each Commissioner by letter . . . each month . . . a summary of all hydrographic data then available . . . pertaining to [deliveries and storage of water under the Compact.]*

(4) *Make such investigations as may be requested by the Commission in aid of its administration of the Compact.*

119

(5) *Act as Secretary to the Commission and submit to the Commission . . . a report of its activities and a summary of all data needed for determination of debits and credits and all other matters pertaining to administration of the Compact.*[8]

The Sabine and Yellowstone Commissions also contract separately with U.S.G.S. for the operation of stream gaging stations. The states party to all four Compacts contribute data from stream gaging stations and from other sources as well; and the Pecos, Sabine, and Rio Grande Commissions also receive considerable help from advisory committees and state advisors to the individual commissioners, who between them perform many of the functions that would otherwise have to be carried on by staff. The Pecos Commission has broader responsibilities for action under its Compact,[9] and thus has, in addition to the arrangements it has made for staff services with U.S.G.S., hired an employee of its own—the Action Program Director. He is concerned solely with the Water Salvage and Salinity Alleviation Program of the Commission, however, and not with the entire range of Commission activity. But in a sense, he has served as a public relations and contact man for the Commission, and he has been available for engineering advice and assistance.

All of the other compact agencies now operating in the United States have hired at least one employee. Even the study-recommendatory agencies, and certainly the

[8] Rules and Regulations for Administration of the Rio Grande Compact, *Thirteenth Annual Report of the Rio Grande Compact Commission* (1951), 23.

[9] See Ch. V, 161, below.

operating agencies, have found that the success of their programs depends on daily, sustained attention and application, which neither the most conscientious commission by itself nor the staff of related state and federal agencies can be expected to give. Thus even the Northeastern Interstate Forest Fire Protection Commission, which has no administrative functions to perform in connection with its work, has employed a minimal staff. The Forest Fire Commission is solely a coordinating agency, whose main purpose is served by the meetings of the Commission itself. Through its meetings, the people in the compacting states most concerned with forest fire protection are brought together and presented with regular opportunities to work out cooperative arrangements. Whatever agreements are reached at Commission meetings are carried out in the states by state officials. The Compact did not endow the Commission with any powers to act. Even so, the Commission found it necessary to employ a part-time executive secretary to provide interim liaison among the several Commissioners, to handle the planning of each Commission meeting, and to supervise the preparation of an annual report and a quarterly newsletter as well as a training program for fire fighters.

The staffs of most of the study-recommendatory agencies are very small. As of July, 1957, the total number of full-time employees of each study-recommendatory agency was as follows:

Atlantic States Marine Fisheries Commission   2
Bi-State Development Agency   2

Because the numbers are so few, no formal philosophy of personnel administration has been developed by most study-recommendatory agencies. The Western Interstate Commission for Higher Education has stated a personnel policy, but it relates solely to staff participation in the development of policy. In the words of its 1956 *Annual Report,*

The central office staff is extremely small. The Commission prefers to operate through consultants and specialists employed on an interim basis for the particular work at hand. The Commission also relies heavily on advisory committees and study groups. This is by deliberate design.[10]

The Board of Commissioners of the Bi-State Development Agency have adopted the policy of "maintaining only a small staff of employees and carrying out its work, insofar as is possible, by the use of outside consultants. In this manner it is expected that its work will be done at the least cost and without the ever-growing permanent staff which too often follows the establishment of a new government department." [11] Generally, however, no such policy is needed, not only because budgetary limitations keep staff small but also because none of the responsibilities of the study-recommendatory agencies requires a large staff.

Although they have not developed a personnel policy, the study agencies are typically much concerned with staffing. Virtually every questionnaire returned to the authors of this study and every compact official who was interviewed stressed the care taken both to obtain the best personnel possible in the first place and then to retain it. In most formal meetings of the compact agencies some attention is devoted to personnel, usually in connection with the approval of the budget. In all the study-recommendatory agencies salary is the largest item in the budget and has consistently been increased over the years.

[10] Western Interstate Commission for Higher Education, *Annual Report* (1956).
[11] *Official Manual, State of Missouri, 1955–1956* (Jefferson City, 1956), 297.

The personnel power of course lies with the appointed compact officials, and some of the study-recommendatory agencies exercise it directly. A few agencies, such as the Interstate Sanitation Commission and the Western Interstate Commission for Higher Education, have established a standing personnel committee. In most cases, however, once an executive officer has been chosen, the selection and control of other personnel is delegated to him. In a few of the larger study-recommendatory agencies, there is a further delegation by the executive officer to an assistant in charge of clerical personnel. A formal designation of responsibility for personnel is not particularly important, however, because in all the study-recommendatory agencies the whole matter of personnel is kept informal. In each case, a slightly different arrangement has evolved. The turnover rate is very low, testifying to the fact that there is general satisfaction.

In general the staff hired by the study-recommendatory agencies can be divided into executive (professional) people on the one hand and clerical people on the other. While the services of the latter are not unimportant, their positions and circumstances of employment are not different enough from those of similar types of personnel employed in other situations to warrant extensive discussion. Suffice it to say that, for the most part, their appointment and tenure are in the hands of the executive director of the agency, that their salary range is roughly equal to and in some cases higher than that in comparable jobs in other governmental agencies and in private business, and that the other conditions of their employment vary in no way very greatly from the common pattern for such jobs.

The most important staff position is of course that of the executive director,[12] who is almost invariably a person professionally trained in the particular field of the compact concerned. He is chosen by the commission or board and is ordinarily the only employee so chosen. None of the compact agencies makes use of a formal application and examination system. Nor does any compact save the New England Interstate Water Pollution Control Compact restrict the commission in its choice, and that compact merely states the obvious, that the secretary "shall be a professional engineer versed in water pollution." [13] Choice is made on the basis of a thorough canvass of suitable candidates and personal interviews with the most likely ones. The Ohio River Valley Water Sanitation Commission, for example, screened some thirty candidates before choosing its first and only executive director, Edward J. Cleary.[14]

The professional qualifications desired of the director differ according to the field in which he must work. Usually the men chosen as chief executive officers of compact agencies have had considerable experience with the problems the compacts were meant to meet. Robert

[12] The executive officer is variously called Executive Secretary, Executive Director, Director, Secretary, Engineer-Secretary, Executive Director-Chief Engineer, and Secretary-Treasurer.

[13] New England Interstate Water Pollution Control Compact, Article IV.

[14] Ohio River Valley Water Sanitation Commission, *First Annual Report, 1948–49*, p. 9.

H. Kroepsch, Executive Secretary of the New England Board of Higher Education, for example, had had a career in teaching and academic administration in his region.

Several executive directors had earlier in their careers been involved in one capacity or another with work in connection with their own or related compact agencies. Thus the present director of the Interstate Commission on the Potomac River Basin, Ellis S. Tisdale, before his appointment to that post, July 1, 1955, had been Chief Engineer of the West Virginia State Health Department and Chairman of the West Virginia State Water Commission. In both capacities his main responsibilities concerned pollution control, in the execution of which he was brought into close contact with the Ohio River Valley Water Sanitation Commission. In addition, he had served as a U.S. Public Health Service officer, where his duties included work on the Ohio River Pollution Survey for the Ohio River Commission. He was thus uniquely qualified to become director of a sister agency.

Increasingly, as compact agencies have gained years and built up some depth in staff, there has been a tendency to promote from within the ranks. When John E. Ivey resigned in 1957 as Director of the Southern Regional Education Board, Robert C. Anderson, Ivey's chief assistant, was named to take his place. And recently, Lawrence R. Alley, Assistant Executive Secretary of the Interstate Oil Compact Commission, was chosen to succeed Earl Foster as Executive Secretary when Judge Foster was moved up to General Counsel for the Commission.

Staffing and Operations

The tenure of the executive officers is surprisingly long. Earl Foster held his post with the Interstate Oil Compact Commission from the establishment of the Commission in 1935 until January, 1958. The first Secretary of the New England Interstate Water Pollution Control Commission is still serving, as is the first Executive Director-Chief Engineer of the Ohio River Valley Water Sanitation Commission and the first Secretary-Treasurer of the Gulf States Marine Fisheries Commission. Although there have been replacements in other agencies due to retirements, deaths, and resignations, by and large turnover has been very low. It appears that these officers, once appointed, have looked upon themselves as career employees of their commissions and have not used their positions as stepping-stones to other jobs. Thus there has been a great deal of stability in the direction of most compact programs.

One reason for the low turnover rate is no doubt the salaries attached to the position. The salaries for executive directors of the study-recommendatory agencies range from $7500 to $17,500 and average over $10,000 a year. Such salaries, coupled with travel expenses and such fringe benefits as health and retirement insurance, are comparable to top salaries in state and federal government service and are at least competitive with the salaries of those men in industry who might be qualified and interested in such positions. In addition, they are generally commensurate with the salaries received by their professional counterparts in other fields of activity, and thus bring satisfaction.

Another reason for the high degree of stability among

the executive directors is no doubt the nature of the jobs. The agencies act through the director's office; very often a program is conceived by him and he then is given the opportunity to carry it out. Between commission meetings, the actual functioning of the agency depends on him. Very seldom are the details of the job spelled out for him. The by-laws of both the Southern Regional Education Board and of the New England Board of Higher Education assign the Director responsibility for "recommending general policies and program plans to the Board, and within the limits of policies and programs approved by the Board [responsibility] for the development and execution of the Board's functions." [15] And the Rules and Regulations of the Atlantic States Marine Fisheries Commission merely state that the Secretary-Treasurer "shall be the executive officer of the commission and perform all the duties customarily performed by a secretary and a treasurer." [16] Such assignments leave a great deal to the man's initiative and imagination.

Moreover, an executive director's job provides an opportunity to work both with people and with ideas. Every executive officer has to "sell" the commission's program to states, municipalities, industries, Congress, and the general public. The Director-Chief Engineer of the Interstate Sanitation Commission is not the only executive officer who "spends half his time making sure

[15] By-Laws, Southern Regional Education Board, Article VI, sec. 3; By-Laws, New England Board of Higher Education, Article VI, sec. 3.
[16] Rules and Regulations, Atlantic States Marine Fisheries Commission, Article IV, sec. 3.

that the problem is understood by the people" in the Compact area.[17] All of his counterparts in other agencies have as much opportunity to exert their abilities as leaders. Because most of the compact agencies work in areas where there are no well-worn paths, every director has the feeling of discovery and invention which does not often come to an employee in ordinary government or industrial jobs.

Finally, the work of the executive officers of the compact agencies is full of variety. The Executive Director-Chief Engineer of the Ohio River Valley Water Sanitation Commission lists his responsibilities as follows, and their breadth is typical:

Direction of administrative, technical and public relations activities; preparation of proposals on policy and execution of control; budgeting and distribution of funds; organization of content and layout of engineering, annual and other reports; development of news releases, speeches [and] articles; coordination of activities with states, federal agencies and other groups allied to commission interests; Engineering Committee and Commission agenda, Kettering project on toxicity; robot-monitor station project; technical-data file assembly and maintenance; quality criteria assembly and file.[18]

In some cases, the director is concerned in addition with

[17] *Cleaning Up the Doorway to America*, 5.
[18] "ORSANCO Staff Organization and Responsibilities— January, 1957" (a worksheet supplied to the authors by Edward J. Cleary).

staff development and direction, office management, and legal matters. Such a job most capable men find exciting and interesting, as well as rewarding.

In the smaller compact agencies, the director himself is the only professional employee. His only assistants are his secretary and perhaps part-time clerical help. In such cases, however, he is not so isolated as might appear. Many, and often all, of the commissioners to whom he is responsible are experienced, and the director's relations with them are usually close and enable him to turn to them as often as he needs. In addition, the small agency necessarily works with state and federal officials in the same area of action, and generally he finds them to be very cooperative. The annual reports of all the study-recommendatory agencies are full of expressions of gratitude for their assistance. The director also receives help from advisory committees established by the commission or, in some instances, by himself and from consultants hired for express purposes. Finally, the several directors themselves form a community and offer each other a great deal of help and encouragement. For instance, the directors of both the Western Interstate Commission for Higher Education and the New England Board of Higher Education were assisted a great deal in the early days of their operations by the Director of the Southern Regional Education Board; and the secretary-treasurers of the Atlantic and Gulf States Marine Fisheries Commissions regularly exchange information and material.

Eight of the study-recommendatory commissions have permitted directors to employ additional professional staff members to assist them. Thus the Director of the

Interstate Commission on the Potomac River Basin is assisted by a full-time writer; the Executive Secretary of the Interstate Oil Compact Commission, by a general counsel and a director of technical services (who doubles as assistant executive secretary); the Director of the Interstate Sanitation Commission, by a general counsel, two full-time and one part-time administrative assistants, four technical employees to perform engineering and laboratory work, and three field employees; the Executive Secretary of the New England Board of Higher Education, by a research associate; the Executive Director-Chief Engineer of the Ohio River Valley Water Sanitation Commission, by an assistant executive director, two engineers, a chemist-biologist, a part-time pollution consultant, and an office manager and treasurer; the Engineer-Secretary of the Upper Colorado River Commission, by an administrative assistant and two engineers; and the Executive Director of the Western Interstate Commission for Higher Education, by an assistant director, a consultant on nursing education, and a part-time research assistant. The Southern Regional Education Board has the most elaborate staff among the study-recommendatory agencies. In addition to the Director, there are four Associate Directors—for Development, Regional Programs, Mental Health Training and Research, and Research—and about twelve persons under their direction.

Just as the commissioners themselves do not make use of any formal recruitment, testing or placement system for the director, so do none of the directors follow any formal procedure in hiring their assistants. When a new professional position is created on an agency staff (such as the proposed addition of a full-time Consultant on Mental Health for the Western Interstate Commission for Higher Education), or when a vacancy occurs in an existing position, the director begins personal inquiries and may occasionally solicit applications. On the basis of recommendations received and personal interviews, he then makes a decision. In some cases, approval of the appointment by the board or commission may be required, but it is usually a matter of form. Once employed, professional staff members are regarded as permanent. Probationary periods are not used, and personnel regulations and procedures are kept at a minimum for such employees. None of the agencies has even a formal promotion schedule for professional employees. The annual review of the salary items in the budget, however, assures attention to promotion possibilities. For directors are aware that the passage of time makes each employee more valuable because he becomes acclimated to compact work and familiar with its peculiarities and that it is to the director's distinct advantage to keep those of his professional assistants who prove satisfactory, rather than train new ones. Only in the case of the Southern Regional Education Board is the staff so large that the Director himself is not directly concerned with each employee's work and training. Thus promotion, at least in salary if not in rank, is common practice. Salary scales for such employees are generally as high or higher than comparable jobs in the state and federal governments. As a result, as with the directors themselves, the turnover rate of professional employees of compact agencies is very low.

Few of the other formal personnel appurtenances of larger governmental agencies are adhered to with any degree of regularity by the study-recommendatory agencies. Retirement, health insurance, and life insurance plans are not practicable for agencies with as few employees as most of the study-recommendatory agencies, although the Southern Regional Education Board has inaugurated a comprehensive program covering all three. By special legislation urged on the 85th Congress, in particular by the members of Congress from Delaware and New Jersey, employees of all interstate agencies were made eligible for social security coverage, so at least that protection is assured them.[19]

In-service training has not been formally instituted by most of the agencies. In a sense, however, some is carried on informally every time the director introduces a new staff member to his duties. Nor are rigid job classifications adhered to very closely. At one time or another, every staff member may perform a number of different functions. Employee relations do not constitute the problem they do in larger operations. No separation has developed between the commissioners, the directors, and the staffs. On the contrary, there is free and frequent intercourse and exchange among all three. Having chosen the executive officer carefully, and having confidence that he will exercise the same care in selecting his

[19] Public Law 226, August 30, 1957, 85th Congress, 1st Session.

assistants, none of the study-recommendatory commissions hesitates to let staff propose and dispose within wide limits.

Staff members attend commission meetings—in fact, they often assist in preparing the agenda—and they are called upon during meetings for advice and ideas. They are there when policy decisions are made, so they know and understand fully what is expected of them as they carry out the policy. During the intervals between commission meetings, staff members participate in the same way in sessions of executive and financial committees. So simple and direct are the operational procedures in most cases that none of the remoteness from the policy level that necessarily characterizes the staff members of most other governmental agencies exists in the compact agencies. The professional staff (and often the stenographic and clerical personnel as well) of most of the compact agencies are fully involved and feel responsible for commission action. This remarkable *esprit de corps* alone goes far toward explaining the significant accomplishments of the study-recommendatory agencies.

Perhaps the only other governmental agency which can be compared in these respects to compact agencies is the Tennessee Valley Authority. Harry L. Case, long-time personnel director of TVA, remarked recently that there was something about the "administrative environment of TVA" which had important effects on the attainment of the Authority's objectives.[20] Case's remarks apply with equal pertinence to most compact agencies:

[20] Harry L. Case, *Personnel Policy in a Public Agency: The TVA Experience* (New York, 1955), 5.

Staffing and Operations

The program . . . of [TVA] *is at once both great and simple. It is great in the sense that it envisages a co-ordinated approach of federal, state and local agencies, groups, and individuals to furthering the development . . . of the Tennessee Valley . . . for the benefit of the people of the region and the nation. By the same token, it is simple and intelligent, because the program revolves about a central idea which can be grasped by the . . . plain worker, as well as by the sophisticated student of economics or political science. This possibility of com-prehending what the job is about, and of being able to see the actual results as worth while . . . gives meaning to the employees' work and provides a source of enthusi-asm and pride.*[21]

Case goes on to comment that generally public servants are given too little responsibility and are not enough in-volved in the total task of their agency to enlist their greatest productivity, but notes that this has not been true of TVA. Nor is it true of most of the employees of compact agencies. What Case saw to be true in regard to TVA employees is just as true of the employees of compact agencies: "Able and imaginative men and women [are] attracted to a program where things [are] being done, responsibility assumed, and decisions made. And these men and women have grown, often beyond their own expectations and the expectations of those who appointed them, in this healthy atmosphere of responsi-bility." [22]

[21] *Ibid.*   [22] *Ibid.*, 118.

135

While these conclusions are valid particularly with regard to the staff of study-recommendatory agencies, they are not totally inapplicable with regard to one or two of the operating agencies. The study-recommendatory agencies, however, by their very nature chiefly involve research and planning—mental as opposed to physical, staff as opposed to line, activities, the kind of activities that arouse interest and excitement in those engaged in them. On the other hand the employees of all the operating agencies save the Waterfront Commission of New York Harbor are chiefly line personnel, whose work is mainly physical—bridge operation and maintenance, park development, and policing, for example. It is hard to imagine a toll collector on the Rouses Point Bridge feeling personally responsible for and involved in the success of the Lake Champlain Bridge Commission in the same sense that the average professional staff member of, say, the Western Interstate Commission for Higher Education does.

The operating compact agencies have, therefore, a personnel situation which differs markedly from that of either the technical or the study-advisory agencies. They more closely resemble other governmental and private enterprises. They are, like all compact agencies, exempt from the civil service laws of the party states and are thus freer to develop their own personnel systems than other types of agencies. For the most part, however, their functions are routine, and their employees are not significantly different from those engaged in the same type of work elsewhere.

Three of the operating agencies are very small and

concerned solely with operating established facilities. Their staff is entirely line, their duties set by the kind of facility involved. In none are professional employees or staff services, as opposed to line functions, required. The Tennessee-Missouri Bridge Commission operates the Tiptonville ferry across the Mississippi River at Tiptonville, Tennessee. In addition to its Secretary, the Commission employs nine men in the ferry operation, and, when traffic is at its peak in the summer, usually adds two more. The secretary serves as manager of the ferry operations. He hires the employees himself, "the requirements being that they be at least 21 years of age, sober, reliable and able to take direction." [23] The ferry pilots must in addition be licensed by the U.S. Coast Guard, and the Coast Guard inspects the Commission's equipment at least twice a year. The employees are paid the going rates for ferry personnel on the Mississippi from the earnings of the ferry. With so small an operation, no formal personnel system is needed.

The Lake Champlain Bridge Commission operates the Lake Champlain Bridge between Crown Point, New York, and Chimney Point, Vermont, and the Rouses Point Bridge, between Rouses Point, New York, and Alburg, Vermont. Each bridge is operated separately under the direction of a bridge superintendent, who is hired by the Commission and is responsible to it. Each bridge requires five toll collectors, who are also hired by the Commission. Though a merit system has not been formally established, political appointments are not made

[23] J. F. Patterson, Secretary, Tennessee-Missouri Bridge Commission, to Richard H. Leach, April 28, 1958.

and, once employed, the collectors are assured of the jobs as long as their work remains satisfactory. The jobs are routine, and each superintendent is empowered to handle the men assigned to him at his discretion. Salaries are of course set by the Commission and are roughly equivalent to those set for employees of other bridges and toll highways in New York.

The Maine-New Hampshire Interstate Bridge Authority operates a toll bridge for vehicular, railroad, and other traffic over the Piscataqua River between Kittery, Maine, and Portsmouth, New Hampshire. The Authority personnel consists of the Executive Secretary, who is charged with the responsibility of operating the bridge and its facilities "in the most efficient and economical manner possible in order to provide sufficient funds from its toll revenue and other income to pay the cost of maintaining, repairing and operating the Bridge and its approaches, to pay the principal of and the interest on the bonds as they become due . . . and to create reserves for such purposes." [24] He is assisted by approximately twenty permanent and ten part-time employees, whom he selects by screening applications filed with the Authority. All of the employees are engaged in toll collection, maintenance, or repair. In addition, the Authority employs engineering and other professional services on a fee basis when needed. As with the other two bridge commissions, salaries are determined by the Authority and personnel matters are kept simple and informal, no rigid procedures

[24] Raymond E. Morrow, Executive Secretary, Maine-New Hampshire Interstate Bridge Authority, to Richard H. Leach, April 15, 1958.

for recruitment, testing, placement, probation, job classification, or promotion being adhered to.

The four remaining operating agencies are the giants of the compact world.[25] Three of them—the Palisades Interstate Park Commission, the Waterfront Commission of New York Harbor, and the Delaware River Port Authority—employ several hundred employees each, and the fourth—the Port of New York Authority—employs several thousand. Thus for all of them, but especially for the Port of New York Authority, a more systematic personnel arrangement is required than for the other compact agencies. Even so, exercising the freedom each has to develop its own concept of personnel administration, they have created distinctive systems. There are, however, a few common elements.

As is the case with the study-recommendatory agencies, the executive officer of each operating agency is the most important member of the staff. The position is even more attractive than it is in the study agencies, and all four executive officers are outstanding in their fields. A. K. Morgan of the Palisades Interstate Park Commission, Joseph K. Costello of the Delaware River Port Authority, and Austin J. Tobin of the Port of New York Authority have been with their agencies long enough to leave the stamp of their personalities upon them. Be-

[25] The Breaks Interstate Park Commission is also an operating agency, having functioned since 1954. Buildings are still under construction, as are a water system, roads and a parking area. A Park Superintendent was employed on April 1, 1958, and when the Park is ready to be opened, additional staff will then be employed. Until that time, no personnel system can be expected to develop.

cause of the scope of their programs, the directors of the operating agencies must be assisted by fairly sizable executive and administrative staffs. Even though all the agencies fight hard against it, the almost inevitable result is a fairly sharp dividing line between "management" and "workers," a situation which does not arise in the study-recommendatory agencies. Again, although the study-recommendatory agencies make little use of the paraphernalia of formal personnel administration, the four operating agencies are forced to adopt much of it. Employment on the basis of examination has been adopted by the Port of New York and Palisades, but many of the other standard features of private and governmental personnel administration—in-service training, job classification, regular salary increments, for example —have been adopted by all four.

Nevertheless, each of the operating agencies is conscious of its position as the creature of a compact and of the opportunities that position gives it with respect to personnel and program, and each has worked hard to develop an appreciation for it among its employees. The high morale of the personnel of the two Port Authorities and of the Waterfront Commission of New York Harbor is one of the first things to be observed in any study of them. Finally, as comprehensive as their staff arrangements are, even the operating agencies find it expedient or necessary to go outside their own personnel for many services, just as the study-recommendatory agencies do. Advisory committees, the cooperation of state and federal agencies, the use of consultants, have all at one time or another been as important to the operating agencies as they are to the study-recommendatory agencies.

Because their personnel systems are different, it is necessary to look at each of the operating agencies briefly in turn. The Palisades Interstate Park Commission has been in operation under its Compact since 1937 and today employs 259 people. As of March, 1958, its staff picture was as follows:

Palisades Interstate Park Commission

	Police	Maintenance and operations	Administrative Engineering & Clerical
Employees in New York	57	97	45
Employees in New Jersey	26	22	12
Totals	83	119	57

With such a staff, over 85% of which is employed in non-administrative positions, a large degree of regularization has been necessary. The Palisades Interstate Park Commission, however, has followed a unique system in the management of its personnel. Employees are considered in different lights for different purposes. For purposes of administration and direction, all employees are considered to be employees of the Commission. All employees are hired by the Commission on the basis of standard examinations; and, though formally all employees serve at the Commission's pleasure, in practice a merit system is in effect. But under its Compact the Commission operates under New York laws in New York and under New Jersey laws in New Jersey. Thus in general, for the police and maintenance and operations personnel, the personnel procedures of the New York Department of Civil Service are followed for employees in New York and those of the New Jersey Department of Civil Service for employees in New Jersey. Those who work in New York are paid out of New York funds at prevailing New York Civil Service rates, and they are considered to be employees of New York for purposes of retirement, health insurance, workmen's compensation, unemployment insurance, and the employer's contribution to social security. A corresponding arrangement applies to the employees who work in New Jersey. There are a number of differences between the two civil service systems. New Jersey has no unemployment insurance system or health plan for its employees, but New York does. Moreover, salary scales for New York employees are generally a little higher than those set for New Jersey employees. A Commission police captain on the New York side may receive from $6140 to $7490 per annum, and an assistant superintendent from $6780 to $8250, while the men in the same jobs in New Jersey receive between $5940 and $7140 as a police captain and $6660 to $7860 as an assistant superintendent. Fortunately the differences do not seem to have created serious grievances.

The administrative personnel are under the Commission itself. They are paid out of the Commission's own funds, and the Commission pays for their social security, retirement, and unemployment and health insurance itself. The professional and executive personnel thus function under what amounts to a third personnel system.

All personnel and staff functions are under the supervision of the General Manager. The emphasis of staff work is of course upon operation and maintenance; and the administrative, engineering, and headquarters clerical staff is thus quite small and operates directly under the General Manager. He delegates to park superintendents responsibility for operating and maintaining each of the parks under the Commission's control. Police functions are entrusted to a chief, who reports directly to the General Manager. The police force is organized along usual police lines, and police units in the two states meet the general standards of police personnel in both states.

The Waterfront Commission of New York Harbor, also created by a compact between New York and New Jersey, has on the other hand developed its own personnel system, totally independent of the party states. Unlike the Palisades Commission, which is concerned primarily with maintaining and operating park facilities and thus employs chiefly non-professional people, the Waterfront Commission's staff is in the main composed of "white-collar" and professional employees, a great many of them lawyers and trained investigators. The Commission was created to eliminate criminal and corrupt practices on the New York waterfront and to regularize the employment of waterfront labor. Thus its "operating" personnel are specially recruited and chosen for the particular job at hand. The present Executive Director, Michael J. Murphy, for example, is on leave from the Police Department of the City of New York, in which he holds the rank of Inspector. Just prior to coming to the Commission, he was commanding officer of the New York Police Academy, and many of the members of the staff have similar professional backgrounds and experience. To recruit such a staff requires a flexible and individually fitted personnel policy, and the Commission has developed one tailor-made for the job.

For the fiscal year 1958, the Commission's table of organization showed a total of 278 employees, distributed among five divisions as follows:

Operating Divisions		259
Division of Law and Enforcement	54	
Division of Investigation	67	
Division of Licensing and Employment Centers	113	
Division of Administration	25	
Executive Division		19

The Commission selects the Executive Director, who, subject to the Commission's approval, then chooses the operating division directors. Each division director in turn selects his own employees with the approval of the Executive Director and the Commission. Tenure is not guaranteed, but because of the nature of most of the jobs and because the Commission has adopted such liberal personnel policies, good performance has been no problem. After a survey of salaries paid for similar job classifications by private industry and other governmental agencies, the Commission established a salary grade plan providing for automatic increments over a three-year period; merit increases are also given when appropriate.

Promotion is from within whenever it is possible, and liberal employees benefits have been granted. All employees are under social security and participate in group hospitalization, medical, and life insurance plans.

The Executive Director is charged with administering the activities of the Commission. He is assisted in managing the actual operations of the Commission, of course, by the Division Director and in the duties of his own office by a General Counsel, a Director of Public Relations, and the Secretary of the Commission. The two Commissioners themselves are very active in the Commission's work, meeting regularly twice a week. The line between Commission and the executive staff is virtually non-existent.[26]

The Delaware River Port Authority and the Port of New York Authority employ the largest staffs among the compact agencies and as a result have developed the most formal personnel systems. As of December 31, 1957, the Delaware River Port Authority employed 416 people, a 57.5% increase over the number it had on the payroll a year earlier. During 1957, the Authority opened its second facility, the Walt Whitman Bridge between Philadelphia and Camden, and consequently required a large increase in its operating personnel. To date, the Authority has not found a personnel department to be necessary. The Authority itself, especially through its standing committee on Continuity of Employment, however, has standardized employment and personnel forms and procedures for all the departments, and each depart-

[26] See Ch. V, 187–95 below, for a detailed case study of the Waterfront Commission.

ment head is responsible for personnel matters to the Executive Director. No written or oral qualifying examinations are given for employment. The operating department chiefs rely instead on interviews and a 120-day probationary period to find satisfactory personnel. No one with a criminal record may be employed, and employees must be as nearly as possible equally divided among the two party states. Each employee signs an agreement, which clarifies his relation to the Authority and his rights as an employee. The agreement states the exact annual salary, and by his signature the employee accepts it and agrees to work for the Authority subject to the following conditions:

1. *The term of employment is during good behavior and depends on the employee's efficiency.*
2. *Employees shall not be discharged or suspended for more than 30 days except for inefficiency, incapacity, or "conduct detrimental to the interest and success of the enterprise, and then only after written . . . charges. . . ."*
3. *The established salary may not be reduced except in the interests of economy and efficiency, and any reduction shall be general.*
4. *All employees shall refrain from political activity.*
5. *The Authority reserves the right to abolish positions but agrees that longevity shall be considered upon releasing employees.*

No formal promotion schedule has been adopted, nor have automatic salary increments been instituted. Promotions and salary raises originate with the operating department, must be approved by the Executive Director and the Executive Committee of the Authority, and finally embodied in an Authority resolution. Salaries in general are good, and other employee benefits, such as insurance and pension arrangements, are attractive, with the result that there were only twenty-six separations from the Authority's service during 1957.

The bulk of the Authority's staff is employed in one of the operating Departments—Police, Toll, Maintenance, Electrical, and Highway. In order to assure skilled personnel in all these areas, as well as in stenographic and clerical work, the Authority carries on a considerable in-service training program. The Authority is also charged with responsibility for developing the Port of Philadelphia, which requires that an important, though numerically small, part of the staff be engaged in research and planning activities. They and the Authority's administrative personnel are recruited in the same way as operating employees, and are subject to the same terms of employment. The entire staff is under the general supervision of the Executive Director, and although the Authority is still young, an excellent working relationship on all staff levels has already come into being.

The Port of New York Authority employed over 4200 persons in 1956, more than the total number of employees of the states of Nevada and Wyoming and only slightly less than the total number employed by Vermont and North Dakota.[27] As a result, it has developed a com-

[27] In October, 1956, Nevada employed only 2,551 persons, Wyoming, 3,904, Vermont, 5,027, and North Dakota, 6,352.

prehensive formal personnel system which has come to be regarded over the years as a model system for governmental agencies. Because that system has been so well described both by the Authority itself[28] and by outside observers,[29] it does not need extensive discussion here. Unlike all its sister compact agencies and more like the practice followed in private business than in government, a Personnel Department is an integral part of the Authority's organization. (See Chart I.) But if the Personnel office is recognized "as an important staff adjunct to the management and an important service to the line officials," the "responsibility for personnel matters" has been equated with "the total job of management," according to one commentator. He adds, "Personnel responsibilities are regarded as something which line officials from the Executive Director down must exercise and cannot delegate in their entirety to the Personnel Office."[30]

The Authority has also formalized a personnel policy, which, in the words of its *Guide for Port Authority Personnel*, can be summarized as follows:

In recognition of the high standards of performance and conduct required of its employees, it is the policy of the

The Book of the States 1958–59 (Council of State Governments, 1958), 149.

[28] See A *Selected Bibliography 1921–1956* (Port of New York Authority, 1956), 37, for a list of Authority and other publications on personnel.

[29] See especially Edgar B. Young, "Personnel Administration in the Port of New York Authority," *Public Personnel Review*, VII (July, 1946), 132–40.

[30] *Ibid.*, 134.

CHART I

Personnel Organization in the Port of New York Authority

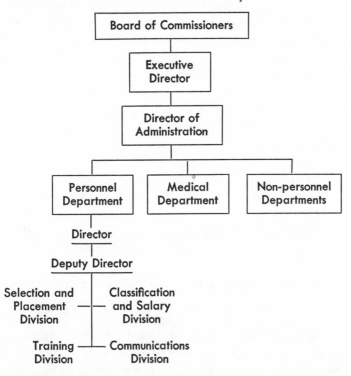

Port Authority to provide opportunities, security, and working conditions that will enable employees to find satisfaction in their jobs and success in their careers.

To assure that this basic idea will be carried out, personnel policies and procedures have been adopted. These policies are concerned with a multitude of things, among them that employees will have tenure of office; that merit will govern selection and promotion; that preferential consideration will not be accorded on account of political or other influence; that salaries will be equal for equal work; that adequate vacations, sick leave, pensions and other employee benefits will be provided; that the best possible employee relations will be maintained.[31]

Elaborate job classification is necessary. In 1957, the Authority reported 639 different kinds of jobs, divided into five main categories:

Maintenance and operating employees	1486
Police	1071
Clerical	759
Technical and engineering	350
Professional, administrative and executive	589

Continuous attention must be devoted to recruitment—284 new employees were added in 1957—for in spite of a turnover rate which is lower than that in the federal government and than the national all-industry rate, in so large an undertaking natural attrition is sizable. And to make the best use of existing staff, intensive in-service training and management development programs must be carried on.[32] During 1957, 2636 staff members par-

[31] *Guide for Port Authority Personnel* (Port of New York Authority, 1954), 3.

[32] See John D. Foster, "Training at the Port Authority," *Good Government*, LXXI (May-June, 1954), 35–38.

ticipated in one or more of the career development programs offered through the Authority's training programs,
which included 39 job-related technical, professional,
and managerial courses.[33] In addition, promotions must
be handled systematically. During 1957, 3476 candidates
took 136 promotion examinations, and 564 (15% of
the entire staff) passed into higher posts.[34]

The Authority is very conscious that it is a public
service corporation and that a major share of the Authority's success in the public eye depends on the quality
of the service rendered. Thus it has not only adopted
higher salary scales than most public enterprises, but it
also attempts through a variety of means to make work
pleasant. It provides employees with health and life insurance and workmen's compensation; gives them good
food at Authority cafeterias at reasonable prices; permits
them to form employees' associations and encourages
them to adjust any grievances they may have; awards distinguished service and commendation medals for unusual
effort or efficiency; solicits employee suggestions and pays
for those adopted; and supports a number of social and
recreational programs. All this requires a considerable
investment of time and resources, investments of course
not possible in smaller agencies with more limited
budgets.

The Authority's success in the short run may depend
on the service given the public at its existing facilities,
but in the long run it depends on the vision and fore-

[33] The Port of New York Authority, *Annual Report, 1957*,
p. 64.
[34] *Ibid.*

sight of its administrative and professional staff. No other compact agency, or few other government agencies of any kind for that matter, have worked harder to locate and hold such employees. On occasion, the Authority has even used the services of a consulting firm which specializes in searching out executive talent. Its top level salaries are to a degree at least comparable to those which the same men might earn in private industry and are at least sufficient, as Austin J. Tobin, the Authority's Executive Director, hoped, to assure "an atmosphere of integrity, confidence and enthusiasm. . . ." [35] The top twenty staff members and their salaries as of 1957 are as follows:

Title	Salary or Salary Range
Executive Director	$60,000
Assistant Executive Director	35,000
Chief Engineer	40,000
General Counsel	40,000
Comptroller	30,000
Director of Administration	27,000
Director, Aviation Department	30,000
Director, Community Relations Department	17,500
Director, Marine Terminals Department	35,000

[35] Austin J. Tobin, "What the Public Administrator Needs from the Personnel Agency," a speech before the Civil Service Assembly, October 20, 1952 (Mimeographed copy), 11. This is an excellent discussion of the entire personnel problem at the Port of New York Authority.

Staffing and Operations

Director, Operations Services Department	25,000
Director, Port Development Department	30,000
Director, Public Relations Department	27,500
Director, Purchase & Administrative Services Department	23,000
Director, Real Estate Department	30,000
Director, Terminals Department	22,500
Director, Tunnels & Bridges Department	27,500
Medical Director	17,000
Personnel Director	26,000
Secretary	12,000
Treasurer	23,500

Despite the size of its staff, the Port of New York Authority has tried to foster a direct and informal relationship between management and employees and to minimize rigid rules and regulations. Significant policy changes are discussed with employees and their representatives before they are finally pronounced. The employees publish the *Port Authority Diary* once a month, and it features detailed discussions of Authority policies and programs. In addition, to keep supervisors informed, the management publishes *The Management Review*, a weekly report covering major programs and progress. And a copy of the Executive Director's weekly report is sent to department heads and other key staff members.

A Supervisors' Forum is held weekly at which ideas and experiences are exchanged and the advice and guidance of the Personnel Director and his staff are available. In these and other ways, the Authority attempts to tie its employees together with management and to encourage the familial feeling which results in pride of work and high-level performance.

The Port of New York Authority's enterprises are so many and so varied that their management cannot be under the direct supervision of the Executive Director. His office is a complex management team, including, besides the Director of Administration, a Director of Finance, to whom a comptroller's department and a treasury department are directly responsible, and a law department headed by a General Counsel. There are eight operating departments—Engineering, Operations, Port Development, Real Estate, Terminals, Tunnels and Bridges, Marine Terminals, and Aviation—each of which in turn is divided into divisions and offices. With such a complex organization, it is all the more important that the varied elements which constitute the staff be integrated and motivated toward high standards of work. As Austin Tobin has remarked, the Authority's success requires "the development of reasonable and understanding working relationships with its employees." [36]

In assessing the success of compact agencies generally in attaining the goals toward which they were originally directed, the role of the staff must be given due credit. Certainly most of the policy alternatives considered by the agencies have originated with the staff, and although

[36] *Ibid.*, 2.

commissions do disagree and make program decisions not recommended by the staff, these cases are the exception and not the rule. The execution of those program decisions has been carried out almost exclusively by staff, and here their performance records are open to all. Moreover, it has largely been through compact agency staff that the public has come to know about the agencies themselves at all. If most of them lack enforcement powers, they have not really needed them because of the understanding of the problems and the role of the agency in solving them the staff has brought about. The remarkable record of success which American compact agencies have built up in so short a time is explained in large part by their ability to recruit and hold able, dedicated men and women on their staffs. In the work of every compact, as in that of those described in the following chapter, the role of the staff is perhaps the most important part of the story.

5: Interstate Compact Agencies:

Selected Case Studies

Six of the interstate compact agencies have been selected for relatively detailed consideration here. They represent the technical, operating, and study-recommendatory types and therefore range, administratively, from the narrowest to the broadest and most complex of the compact agencies. It happens that four of these agencies are concerned with some phase of conservation, but no inference that interstate compacts are somehow limited in application to this field should be drawn from the case studies. Historically, compact agencies have been identified with conservation, broadly conceived, perhaps because of the large number of water allocation agencies; but nothing strikes the observer more forcefully than the variety of applications to which compacts have been adapted. Moreover, as the case studies will show, some of the compact agencies which are specifically devoted to conservation programs actually perform functions of unexpectedly various kinds.

Selected Case Studies

The Pecos River Commission is presented first as an example of the primarily technical compact agencies, concerned, by and large, with engineering problems and therefore comparatively simple from the administrative point of view. The looseness of the categories under which the compact agencies are considered here may be emphasized again by pointing out that even the water allocation commissions sometimes go beyond merely technical functions when they act as water masters. To determine where water shall go in the light of the consequences for different areas is to operate on a very high plane of public policy. Next, the Atlantic States Marine Fisheries Commission is examined; it too is a conservation agency, but it turns out to be busy with the coordination of biological and oceanographic research.

Then appears the Ohio River Valley Water Sanitation Commission, whose work also centers on a technical problem which must be approached, however, in complex fashion and which involves many activities only indirectly related to controlling stream pollution. The fourth account concerns the Waterfront Commission of New York Harbor, presented as an example of an operating-type compact agency; and the Interstate Oil Compact Commission is then described as a purely study-recommendatory agency without power but with influence proportionate to the scope of its research and the quality of its advice. Finally, the Southern Regional Education Board is discussed as an instance of compact agencies which, although essentially advisory, combine, at least theoretically, some features of the other types and deal with such extremely varied subject matter as to suggest concretely the scope of activities which may be carried on under interstate compacts.

The Pecos River Commission

No interstate issue has been more productive of prolonged quarrels and bitter hostility than the use of the waters of interstate streams, especially among the arid western states, where water is so precious a commodity. In many instances, recourse to the United States Supreme Court has been thought necessary, but interstate compacts have been increasingly relied on to settle water disputes. The Council of State Governments reported that seventeen such compacts were in effect in 1956, not all of which, however, established administrative arms. One of the most successful is the Pecos River Compact between Texas and New Mexico.

The Pecos River rises in the Sangre de Christo Mountains in New Mexico and flows for almost 800 miles southeasterly through New Mexico and Texas before it empties into the Rio Grande River in Texas. It drains a 33,000-square-mile area of high plains and mountains. It normally carries very little water, its flow coming chiefly from mountain snows and artesian sources. It is, however, subject to flash floods, which sometimes reach major proportions. Agriculture in the Pecos Basin has been possible under these conditions only by the development and maintenance of numerous water storage facilities. Over the years the scant waters of the river became fully appropriated, and every proposal for additional storage became the subject of controversy between the two states. Although interim agreements to provide controls against the construction of additional storage facilities were made from time to time, none proved satisfactory for long. Each state was jealous of its authority over the portion of the river within its boundaries, and neither was willing to make the compromises necessary for permanent settlement of the dispute.

If it had not been for the fact that all the while the two states were bickering, the waters of the Pecos were becoming scarcer and decreasing in quality, the logic of a solution by compact might never have been brought home to either state. While storage is the key to the use of the river's waters, the development of adequate storage throughout the basin is hampered by a lack of good reservoir sites, by the steady encroachment of growths of salt cedar—a type of native vegetation which absorbs a great deal of water—and by extremely heavy sedimentation. Moreover, the problem of flood control is complicated. "At the same time the River needs flood control, it is the type of stream that has to survive on its flood waters, which in turn means adequate control for conservation where there is little chance for the necessary reservoir space to accomplish this." [1] To attack all of these problems successfully was admittedly beyond the capacity of either state alone, yet neither state wished to turn them over for solution to the federal government. An interstate compact seemed to be the least disagreeable means of attacking them.

A compact to accomplish these purposes was first drawn up and approved by the legislatures of the two

[1] John H. Erickson, Interstate Stream Engineer, State of New Mexico, to Richard H. Leach, October 8, 1953.

states in 1925, but the governor of New Mexico vetoed that legislature's action. The project then lagged for several years, but in 1933, the New Mexico legislature reconsidered the compact and approved it once again, with amendments and revisions. Final action was never accomplished, however, and the compact was allowed to die quietly.

During 1939 and 1940, the National Resources Planning Board became interested in the Pecos Basin and got the two states to undertake, under its supervision, a joint investigation of the river. In the course of that study, interest in a compact was revived. A Pecos River Compact Commission was subsequently appointed by the governors of the two states and began its negotiations early the next year. Nine meetings were held in all, some of them open. Testimony was taken at all the meetings, and every interested person was allowed to express his point of view. In addition, a five-man Engineering Advisory Committee of water experts was established by the Commission. It made a detailed technical study of the basin and strongly recommended the consummation of a compact. The details of a mutually satisfactory compact were worked out in 1948, and having been approved by Congress the next year, became immediately effective. Probably no other compact has been preceded by such exhaustive study. By the time the final session of the Pecos River Compact Commission was held, all the points at issue between the two states had been resolved, and the expectations of both states were high. The first ten years of the Compact's operation have only served to strengthen the harmony that prevailed in 1948.

Insofar as it is concerned with "the equitable division and apportionment of the use of the waters of the Pecos River." [2] the Pecos River Compact differs only in detail from most of the other water compacts in effect today. Articles III, IV and VI set forth the principles of division and specify the conditions under which each state may use the waters of the river and construct additional storage facilities. Immediately upon acceptance of the Compact, these provisions of course became part of the water law of each state, but the Compact provides a formal guarantee that each state will abide by the law.

Because the party states also had the problem of water salvage in mind when they drafted it, the Pecos River Compact is broader than many similar compacts. Article I sets the stage for a broader range of activities by declaring that an additional purpose of the Compact is "to facilitate the construction of works for, (a) the salvage of water, (b) the more efficient use of water, and (c) the protection of life and property from floods." And Article IV establishes the conditions under which each state may add to its own reservoir capacity in the basin and makes it obligatory for both states to cooperate with each other "to support legislation for the authorization and construction of projects to eliminate non-beneficial consumption of water" and to cooperate with the federal government in devising means of alleviating the salinity conditions in the river.

[2] Pecos River Compact, Article I.

To carry out these purposes, the Compact creates as its administrative arm the Pecos River Commission, consisting of one representative each from New Mexico and Texas, and since federal interests are involved, a representative of the federal government as well. The federal representative is chairman of the Commission without vote. No qualifications are established for membership, nor is a term of office set. Commissioners serve without compensation. The Compact defines the powers of the Commission in detail [3] and is careful to protect the power of the party states in other ways as well. Thus it prescribes the method by which water use under the Compact shall be measured, it permits the Compact's termination at any time by the legislatures of the two states, and it specifies, "Findings of fact made by the Commission shall not be conclusive in any court, or before any agency or tribunal. . . ." [4]

Recognizing that the Commissioners appointed would probably not be free to devote a great deal of time to their duties, the Compact provides that the Commission may employ a secretary as well as such "engineering, legal, clerical, and other personnel as in its judgment may be necessary for the performance of its functions under this Compact." [5] Acting under this authority, the Pecos River Commission has contracted with the U.S. Geological Survey for engineering and clerical services. Under the terms of the contract, the U.S.G.S. operates the twenty-five stream gaging stations required for the administration of the Compact, makes such investigations

[3] *Ibid.*, Article V, d.   [4] *Ibid.*, f.   [5] *Ibid.*, c.

as the Commission requests and reports to the Commission regularly.

An engineer in the Carlsbad, New Mexico, office of U.S.G.S. serves as Commission secretary. He issues calls for the regular meetings and for special meetings when instructed by the chairman, prepares agenda for the meetings of the Commission, keeps the Commission's books and does some of the fiscal work, prepares and distributes the minutes of the meetings, and prepares the annual report, when one is issued.[6] Most of the engineering work for the Commission is done by the Engineering Advisory Committee, composed of specialists in the various phases of water problems, who serve on a per diem basis.

The Commission's work falls into two distinct phases. The first, which is common to all the compact water allocation agencies, relates to ascertaining whether or not the states are abiding by the apportionment provisions of the Compact. Data collected by the U.S.G.S. and supplied by the states themselves are studied by the Commission. If violation of the Compact's terms seems to have occurred, the Commission reports the matter to the proper official of the state concerned. The Commission is not endowed with enforcement power itself but must rely on state officials to correct whatever deviations it finds. The only power the Commission has, once it has reported a violation to the proper state official, is to frame a recommendation on the matter at issue for submission to the state legislature.

[6] Sherman O. Decker, Secretary, Pecos River Commission, to Richard H. Leach, February 19, 1954.

The other phase of the Commission's work combines research and promotion and is peculiar to the Pecos Commission.[7] As early as 1953, a series of ground-water studies was planned and undertaken as was a full-scale investigation of ways to improve the quality of the water in the lower Pecos River by removal of the brine inflow in the vicinity of Malaga Bend. At the same time, the Commission became interested in the possibility of salvaging water by means of a channel through the salt-cedar area of Lake McMillan Delta. Officials of the Bureau of Reclamation, the Departments of Agriculture and Interior, and the Corps of Engineers, as well as of state agencies, assisted the Geological Survey and the Engineering Advisory Committee by providing data. The Commission employed a full-time Program Director to coordinate the studies and correlate the data. The Commission's Legal Committee used the data in drafting a bill proposing what has become its Water Salvage and Salinity Alleviation Program for the Commission's consideration. The Commission accepted the draft and rec-

[7] The Upper Colorado River Commission was also assigned by the Upper Colorado River Compact a broader purpose than mere apportionment. It was directed to secure "the expeditious agricultural and industrial development of the Upper Basin States, the storage of water, and the protection of life and property from floods." (Article I). Like the Pecos Commission, the Upper Colorado River Commission has had two main activities: supervising the apportionment provisions of the Compact, and pushing for the enactment by Congress of the Colorado River Storage Project Bill. That Bill has been enacted into law and the project actually begun. See Neil M. Clark, "Giant of the Colorado," *The Saturday Evening Post*, CCXXX (April 5, 1958), 37 seq., for a description of the nature of the project.

ommended that it be submitted to Congress. The Program Director devoted nearly all his time during the 85th Congress to securing passage of the bill and succeeded early in 1958. An initial appropriation has already been made for the start of the Salinity Program, and one for the Water Salvage Program will probably be forthcoming in the next few years.

The Commission does not visualize a larger role for itself growing out of the adoption of the Program by Congress, however. When the Water Salvage and Salinity Alleviation Program has been completed, the Commission expects to study other problems which stand in the way of the fullest development and use of the River's waters and to prepare and push for the adoption of recommendations for their solution. It would not become an operating agency, even if the Compact permitted it to do so, because the Commissioners believe that the construction and operation of new facilities are properly the functions of the states or the federal government. Its own role it conceives to be that of a combination investigator and catalytic agent.

The Pecos River Commission's budget was originally very small, but with the decision to develop an action program, it was considerably expanded. For fiscal 1956 and 1957, the total budget was $42,250 per annum, $13,000 being allotted to personal services (the salaries of the Program Director and the Commission Secretary-Treasurer, and per diem payments to advisors), $4,000 to travel expenses, $21,000 to contractual expenses (U.S.G.S.), $2,850 to continuation of ground-water studies, and $800 to printing. The funds of the Commission come from both state and federal governments. Article V of the Compact follows the pattern of most water compacts by declaring that all expenses "which are incurred by the Commission incident to the administration of this Compact and which are not paid by the United States shall be borne equally by the two states."

The degree of cooperation over the budget achieved between the two states has been remarkable. At one time, New Mexico bore what seemed to be a very disproportionate share of the Commission's expenses, and this entirely without difficulty or hard feelings. Neither state has been unwilling or hesitant to meet requests for increased appropriations. The federal government has made a considerable contribution to the Commission's activities, but its contribution has by no means been the major portion of the Commission's income. The cost of the U.S.G.S. services, however, is probably more than the Commission is required to pay, and the services of a great many other federal officials and agencies have been freely extended. The support of the federal government, indeed, has been one of the factors which have made the Pecos Commission so successful.

For the Pecos Commission must be rated as a success. The Compact itself was drawn up only after extensive examination of all the factors hindering effective water use in the basin, and it represented the consensus of informed opinion as to the best way to remove them. Thus it was well received at the outset, and the Commission was able to begin operations free from the old grudges which have marred the work of other water allocation agencies and which are particularly characteristic

of the Rio Grande Compact Commission. The Commissioners have been chosen with care and have gone
about their job with the conviction that the Compact
can be effective in solving the water problems in the
basin. The states have scrupulously honored the Compact and done everything to meet the Compact requirements. The Commission has been accepted by water
agencies in both states because it has earnestly respected
the strong feeling of the states that "administration of
their respective water supplies must remain in the states
and cannot be delegated to an overriding Compact
authority." [8]

The Atlantic States Marine Fisheries Commission

All fifteen states on the Atlantic seaboard are parties to
the Atlantic Marine Fisheries Compact of 1940, which
was formulated in an attempt to prevent the further
decline of the great Atlantic shore fisheries. Intense fishing over the years had resulted in a general economic
decline in these fisheries and in the possibility that several of them—particularly the lobster, shad, and sturgeon
fisheries—would be depleted. Yet, because fish are migra-
tory, conservation regulation by individual states, even
where it existed, was not enough to reverse the trend.
Nor could the federal government solve the problem, for
the regulation of shore fisheries is so clearly an example
of state power that Congress is probably barred from
acting at all in that field. The only way, therefore, that
valuable marine species could be preserved, the interests

[8] John H. Bliss, New Mexico Member, Pecos River Commission, to Richard H. Leach, March 23, 1954.

of sportsmen respected, and the livelihood of commercial fishermen insured was through interstate cooperation;[9] or, in the words of the Compact, by "the development of a joint program for the promotion and protection of fisheries and the prevention of the physical waste of the fisheries from any cause." [10]

The Atlantic States Marine Fisheries Commission, created by Article III of the Compact, is composed of three representatives from each party state, one of whom is required to be the executive officer of the state's marine fishery agency, one, a member of the state legislature,[11] and the third, a citizen "who shall have a knowledge of and interest in" marine fisheries and their problems. The Commission thus has forty-five members.

Its size has not imposed a handicap on its operations, however, because for many years the Commission has been subdivided into four Sections dealing with recognized units of the coast which have common fishery interests—the North Atlantic, the Middle Atlantic, the Chesapeake Bay, and the South Atlantic Sections. These

[9] The complete story of the reasons for the Compact, the steps leading up to its formulation, and what the Compact was expected to accomplish is well told by Frederick L. Zimmermann in "Atlantic States Marine Fisheries Compact," *State Government*, XIV (April, 1941), 81–3, and in "Interstate Cooperation and Fisheries," *ibid.*, XV (August, 1942), 159–62.

[10] Atlantic States Marine Fisheries Compact, Article I.

[11] The Compact provides that the Commission on Interstate Cooperation in each state appoint the legislative member; that being impossible, the governor; and if it is constitutionally impossible for a legislator to serve as a member of a Compact commission, that the second member be appointed at the governor's discretion, as is the third member.

divisions are not mutually exclusive. New York often sits in on meetings of the North Atlantic Section, Connecticut with the Middle Atlantic Section, and North Carolina with the Chesapeake Bay Section. The Sections have worked out very well. They allow greater specialization and concentration of interests than would otherwise be possible. The Compact does not set a term of office for the commissioners, nor does it mention the matter of compensation. Originally, the Commission paid the travel expenses of its own members while on Commission business, but this procedure was found difficult to administer. In 1946, therefore, the Commission adopted a resolution requesting the states to provide the expenses of their own commissioners. The Commission as a whole meets in formal session only once a year, but a number of special meetings are held, and the Sections meet independently of the Commission several times a year.

As is the case with most compact agencies, the membership of the Commission has been relatively stable, a nucleus of old members providing a considerable element of continuity in Commission procedure and practice. The Commission's only regular staff members are a full-time secretary-treasurer and his secretary and a part-time adviser. The Compact called for the creation of an over-all Advisory Committee, representative of commercial fishermen and salt water anglers and such other interests as the Commission deemed advisable to have represented, to work with it on its recommendations. In practice, however, the Committee "just did not work. Consequently, to keep within the terms of the Compact

. . . that overall Advisory Committee [was broken up] into an advisory group for each state, leaving it to the individual state to determine how much it wishes to use such advisors." [12] The result has been that advisory groups have not been utilized by the Commission to the extent that they have been by other compact agencies.

The Commission does make frequent use of special committees, however. The members of these committees are lawyers, state legislators, marine scientists, members of state fish and game commissions, or staff members of the U.S. Fish and Wildlife Service, depending on the nature of the particular assignment. Through such committees, the Commission has studied the special problems of striped bass, clams, lobsters, shad, and blue crab, as well as those of several other species. The committees report their findings to the Commission, which then prepares recommendations for action, if it seems warranted, to the state fishery agencies, the state legislatures, the U.S. Fish and Wildlife Service, or Congress. Over the years, a great many of the several committees' recommendations have been converted into practice.

As the frequent appointment of special study committees implies, the Atlantic States Marine Fisheries Commission is concerned chiefly with research and recommendation. The Rules and Regulations under which it operates declare it to be a "fact finding and deliberative body with the power to make recommendations to the member states and to the Congress of the United

[12] Wayne D. Heydecker, Secretary-Treasurer, Atlantic States Marine Fisheries Commission, to Richard H. Leach, July 15, 1954.

States." [13] The Commission discovered almost as soon as it was organized the great dearth and indefiniteness of biological knowledge about the species with which it was concerned, and it has made its chief goal the increase of such knowledge, on the basis of which policy decisions with respect to each species can be made with greater assurance.

Although research is the Commission's main interest, it does not itself engage in research. It did, however, undertake one research project. Under a grant-in-aid from the U.S. Public Health Service, it studied the effect of pollution on the marine fisheries of the Atlantic Coast; but the material did not seem to warrant completion of the project. Since then, the Commission has felt that its proper function is fostering and coordinating research by other agencies. By the terms of the Compact, the U.S. Fish and Wildlife Service is designated as the "primary research agency" of the Commission; and state agencies and organizations of commercial salt water fishermen and salt water anglers also occasionally undertake research at the Commission's suggestion.

An example of the way in which the Commission operates is the procedure it followed in the conduct of its striped bass project several years ago. The project was developed by the Commissions's Striped Bass Committee with the help of the Fish and Wildlife Service. Grants-in-aid were then sought and received under the Dingell-Johnson Act by seven member states, and four other states were encouraged to cooperate with the project

[13] Rules and Regulations, Atlantic States Marine Fisheries Commission, Article I, sec. 2.

through their own fishery agencies. At the Commission's request, the Fish and Wildlife Service provided a single coordinator for the project, whose duty was to assist the states and to carry on certain broad research studies. The project was thus the Commission's idea, resulting from the action of one of its special committees, it was activated by the Commission's efforts in securing the cooperation of the Fish and Wildlife Service and in pointing out sources of financial support to the states, and it culminated in a series of recommendations by the Commission.

It should be noted that contributory reasons to the Commission's decision to abstain from research itself have been a perennial lack of funds and the consequent inability to employ an adequate staff with which to undertake its own research. If funds had been available in sufficient quantity, there is little doubt that the Commission might have developed a research program of its own. But instead, state funds have gone, with the Commission's blessing, to strengthen existing state research facilities and to create new ones, with the result that a great deal more marine research is being undertaken on the state level in the Compact area than ever before.

The Atlantic States Marine Fisheries Commission was originally empowered to draft model laws for the regulation of various species of fish by the several party states. A number of model laws were drafted and recommended to the governors and legislatures of the states, and a few were enacted. The Commission soon concluded, however, that uniform legislation was not practicable because of the great ecological differences and weather variations along a north-south coast and that it might make a greater contribution in other ways. As a result, the emphasis of the Commission's meetings and activities early turned from the formulation of public policy to the collection of scientific data upon which to base sound public policy. The Commission has also been active in advising the state fishery agencies with regard to problems connected with fisheries and improved fishery management practices. It maintains an extensive information file, including a complete index of World Fishery Abstracts and Commercial Fishery Abstracts, which are available for general use and reference. It also performs a clearing-house function in that it keeps up with and disseminates to the member states information on developments in fishery law and regulation throughout the Compact area.

The Commission also serves an educational function. At all meetings of the Commission and of its Sections as well, which are open to the public, problems of the fisheries and approaches to their solution are discussed by some of the leading marine scientists in the United States. In addition, the activities of the marine fishery agencies in the party states are described, a report is given on the current programs of the Fish and Wildlife Service, and comments are made on actions of Congress and of state legislatures and administrative agencies which affect fisheries. Virtually no important aspect of fishery conservation and development is neglected, as those who participate in the Commission's activities attest. Unfortunately, the lack of financial resources has so far prevented the Commission from developing its educational program further and in particular from designing a program for the lay public. The Commission recognizes the long-range value of such a program, however; and its development may be expected when an increased budget can be secured.

The Commission might also be said to be the general watchdog of fishery interests in the Compact area. At each meeting it is common for the Commission to consider matters of current interest and to pass a number of resolutions concerned with fisheries to be sent on to the appropriate executive agency or legislature. Representatives of the Commission appear in behalf of fishery interests before a great many groups, both at home and abroad. They have appeared, for example, before the National Fisheries Institute, conferences called by the U.S. State Department, the Oyster Institute, the U.S. Fish and Wildlife Service, the National Shell Fisheries Association, the American Fisheries Society, and the Association of Attorney-Generals, as well as before state Commissions on Interstate Cooperation. The Commission has submitted memoranda and has testified before Congressional and state legislative committees, and every year it files with the states a summary of legislation it considers necessary in each state to promote and protect fisheries. Together with the Gulf State Marine Fisheries Commission and the Pacific Marine Fisheries Commission, it constitutes an effective voice for fishery interests in the United States.

The budget of the Atlantic Marine Fisheries Commission, as has been suggested, is very small. The Compact does not specify a particular sum to be contributed by the party states. It merely says that the "states party hereto agree to make annual appropriations to the support of the Commission," [14] in proportion to the primary market value of the fisheries products (exclusive of haddock and cod) of each state, no state to contribute less than $200 a year. Later this minimum was voluntarily raised to $590 and then to $700 a year, but for many years it has remained at that figure. The current budget is around $19,700 per annum. The largest amount appropriated by any state is the $4400 appropriated by Massachusetts. Such a budget does not permit much more than the payment of the salaries of the secretary-treasurer and his secretary, fees to the advisors, office expenses, and travel.

By Amendment Number One to the Compact, passed in 1950, the Commission has been authorized to establish regulatory agencies within its framework. The amendment provides that if two or more of the party states so request, the Commission may establish special Sections, consisting of the members of the Commission from the states concerned, to regulate specific fisheries in which the participating states have a common interest. The fishing operations of the citizens and vessels of a state, however, can be regulated only to the extent of the powers specifically delegated by the states to the Section, and then only if the states appropriate funds for the actual operation of the Section. If ever established, such a Section would become a joint regulatory agency of the states which created it, rather than of the Commission

[14] Atlantic States Marine Fisheries Compact, Article XI.

itself. It would be lodged in the Commission's framework merely for administrative convenience.

There is general agreement that the Commission has been useful to the compacting states in a number of ways. It has provided leadership in the development of public policy in a field long neglected and has focussed attention on fishery problems and on the need for research to solve many of them. It has produced teamwork among the states in the conduct of fishery research and has given added impetus to the development of state fishery programs. It must be credited, at least in part, with bringing about increased legislative support for state marine programs. Finally, the Commission has stimulated federal concern for fisheries problems: chiefly through pressure exerted by it and the other fisheries commissions, additional federal funds have been made available in support of state research programs.

The Ohio River Valley Water Sanitation Commission

Two hundred thousand square miles in fourteen states are drained by the Ohio River and its nineteen major tributaries. The entire area has long been thickly populated, highly industrialized, and heavily dependent upon the waters of the Ohio for domestic and industrial use as well as for transportation, recreation, and the generation of electric power. Yet nowhere in the United States was community growth and industrial development allowed to bring "a greater foulness to streams than in the Ohio valley." [15] Vast amounts of untreated sewage were

[15] Ohio River Valley Water Sanitation Commission, *2nd Annual Report* (1950), 5.

freely dumped into the main river and its tributaries daily, as were untold additional gallons of industrial wastes. The result throughout the length and breadth of the valley was an ever more unsanitary, unhealthy, unsightly, unpleasant, and uneconomic river system. By the mid-nineteen thirties, in the words of Paul V. McNutt, then Federal Security Administrator, the pollution problem in the Ohio River valley "overshadowed that of any other drainage basin in the United States." [16]

Because of the diversified nature and sources of pollution and the many governmental agencies which would necessarily be involved in controlling it, the problem was hard to approach. Moreover, the states in the valley were used to inaction. Ohio had let it be known as early as 1908 that "its river cities need not install sewage treatment facilities until communities in other states on the banks of the Ohio did likewise." [17] If such specific declarations of policy were not made by the other states in the valley, they were as inclined as Ohio to let the other fellow take the first step. The steadily increasing industrialization of the region, and the accompanying rise in population, finally made action of some sort imperative. A tentative step toward solution of the larger problem was taken in 1928 when an informal agreement was reached among eleven of the states in the basin to act together to control the discharge of certain taste-producing phenols from coke plants into the rivers. Then came the severe droughts of 1930 and 1934, which so reduced

[16] House Report 2653, 76th Congress, 3rd Session, 2.
[17] Ohio River Valley Water Sanitation Commission, *1st Annual Report* (1948–9), 3.

177

the amount of available water in the rivers that only the most callous could ignore any longer the prevailing stench or overlook the menace it represented to the public health throughout the region.

Under the leadership of the Cincinnati Chamber of Commerce, civic organizations and sanitary authorities in almost every state concerned combined to secure governmental action. Because it was obvious to everyone that successful action on such a matter could only be interstate in character, a regional program of pollution abatement, based on an interstate compact, was considered from the outset. Congress gave impetus to the growing demand for interstate action by authorizing negotiation for a compact in 1936,[18] and shortly thereafter an Ohio River Valley Water Compact Commission was formed to draft an appropriate document. With the help of the Council of State Governments, agreement on the terms of a compact was reached in 1938, and by 1940, Indiana, West Virginia, Ohio, New York, Illinois, and Kentucky had accepted it and Congress had approved it. Certain reservations regarding the participation of Pennsylvania and Virginia had to be removed, however, and it was not until 1948 that Virginia finally accepted its terms. Ninety days later, June 30, 1948, the Compact became effective. Twenty years had gone by since the first interstate action to curb phenol discharges had been taken, and during those years, government officials, industrial representatives, and private citizens in all eight states had taken part in the movement. As a

[18] 49 Stat. 1490 (1936).

178

result, the Compact had a wide circle of friends from the moment of its birth.

Through the Compact, the signatory states pledge themselves to cooperate faithfully with each other in the abatement of existing pollution and in the control of future pollution in the Ohio River Basin and in particular "to enact any necessary legislation to enable each . . . state to place and maintain the waters of said basin in a satisfactory sanitary condition, available for safe and satisfactory use as public and industrial water supplies after reasonable treatment, suitable for recreational usage, capable of maintaining fish and other aquatic life, free from unsightly or malodorous nuisances due to floating solids or sludge deposits, and adaptable to such other uses as may be legitimate." [19]

The Compact does not prescribe how pollution shall be controlled. For this purpose it creates as the agent of the states the Ohio River Valley Water Sanitation Commission, composed of three representatives from each member state and three from the federal government. Although the Compact follows the usual pattern of such instruments in not setting requirements for membership, the states have generally seen to it that their representatives are persons vitally concerned with pollution control in the course of their every-day jobs. Members of state health commissions and of state stream pollution control boards and representatives of industries drawing water from rivers in the basin are most commonly designated as commissioners. The Commission itself meets four

[19] Ohio River Valley Water Sanitation Compact, Article I.

times a year, and throughout the year the program it decides upon is carried out by a small professional staff, consisting in 1958 of an executive director who doubles as chief engineer, an assistant executive director, two sanitary engineers, and a chemist-biologist. The professional staff in turn is served by a small clerical and secretarial staff. The Commission is also assisted in its work by three advisory committees, an Engineering Committee, a Water Users Committee, and an Aquatic Life Committee.

The membership of the Commission and the personnel of the staff have been remarkably stable over the years. Blucher A. Poole, the 1957–58 Chairman of the Commission, for example, had served as a commissioner from Indiana since the establishment of the Commission, and Edward J. Cleary, the executive director, has held his post just as long. The average length of service of all commissioners and staff is over five years.

The Compact does not prescribe in detail the Commission's duties. It does say that the Commission shall study the pollution problem in the basin, make a comprehensive report on the reduction and prevention of stream pollution therein, draft and recommend uniform legislation dealing with pollution to the several states, and consult with and advise state and local officials with regard to particular pollution problems and the construction of sewage treatment plants.[20] In addition, it establishes a floor for the minimum treatment of all sewage dumped into the rivers in the basin. In general, however,

[20] *Ibid.*, Article VII.

it leaves the Commission remarkably free to use its discretion. Guided by the principle that no sewage or industrial waste originating within a signatory state shall adversely affect the use of water by another state, the Commission is free to establish the standards for water quality it believes to be necessary in the different parts of the basin.

This of course constitutes the heart of the Commission's work. Before adequate standards can be set, "it is necessary to ascertain what substances are present in the waters. Then each substance must be studied to determine the maximum concentration that can be tolerated without deleterious effect, beyond which the water is unsuitable for certain uses. Uniform methods of testing polluting substances, particularly industrial wastes, must be established." [21] Therefore, in order to develop "a continuing record of what is happening and to be alerted on pollution potentials the Commission operates a network of 43 water-quality monitor stations" along the rivers of the basin.[22] In addition, the Commission carries on a broad research program. The Commission staff engages in technical studies of its own, and the Commission sponsors research by state, federal, and private agencies. Recently, for example, the U.S. Public Health

[21] Ohio River Valley Water Sanitation Commission, *4th Annual Report* (1952), 7.

[22] Ohio River Valley Water Sanitation Commission, *9th Annual Summary* (1957), 8. Fifteen of the stations are operated by the Water Users Committee of the Commission; the remainder are serviced under a cooperative agreement with the U.S. Geological Survey.

Service undertook at the Commission's request a series of radiation studies; the Kettering Laboratory of the University of Cincinnati contracted to engage in an extensive taste and odor study; and the Biology Department of the University of Louisville began an inventory and evaluation of the aquatic life resources of the Ohio River.

On the basis of such studies, the Commission drafts recommendations for abatement and control. When the Commission decides on a standard for sewage treatment higher than the minimum established by the Compact, or when it seeks to specify treatment for industrial discharges, it must hold a public hearing before it adopts the regulation. If an abatement order is issued, it must have the assent of at least a majority of the Commissioners from a majority of the signatory states as well as the assent of a majority of the Commissioners from the state in which the order is to be issued.

In addition to its basic job of establishing appropriate standards of water quality thoughout the basin, the Commission carries on a number of other programs as well. It coordinates the stream sanitation activities of the several state pollution control agencies and of the three federal agencies concerned in the field—the U.S. Public Health Service, the U.S. Corps of Engineers, and the U.S. Fish and Wildlife Service. It assists each of the party states to strengthen its own anti-pollution laws and machinery. By 1953, when certain amendments to the West Virginia pollution control act became effective, the Commission could report that "each of the states now has . . . adequate legislation to accelerate control action; in two states this required a completely new law," [23] which the Commission helped to formulate.

Another important activity has been the Commission's effort to persuade the industries in the basin to cooperate in a pollution abatement program. Action committees, composed of representatives of management of the different types of industry in the basin, have been established to link the Commission and individual industrial plants. The committees have shown a great deal of initiative and have been very successful. At the same time the committees have performed a great deal of research for the Commission. During 1957, the Steel Committee, for example, inaugurated work on recovery of mill-scale from water and the effects of scale on downstream use. It also undertook a comprehensive survey of the water quality requirements of steel mills.

Finally, the Commission leads a regional crusade for clean streams. It has developed "community-action" materials, prepared exhibits, published handbooks for municipal officials and industrial use, made movies, and presented radio and television shows—all to arouse the people of the valley to the necessity of action. In addition to its informative *Annual Reports*, it makes the findings of all its technical studies widely available as part of an extensive publications program. Its 1957 publications list contained over 35 titles.

The Ohio River Valley Water Sanitation Commission is set apart from most compact agencies by the fact that

[23] Ohio River Valley Water Sanitation Commission, *5th Annual Report* (1953), 4.

it is endowed by its Compact with the power to secure compliance with the standards it sets.[24] Article IX of the Compact makes it the duty of the municipality, corporation, person, or entity to whom the Commission issues an order to comply with it, and the Commission is given power to call on any court of general jurisdiction or on any United States District Court in any of the Compact states to enforce its order by mandamus, injunction, order of specific performance, or some other equally appropriate form of legal action. Ordinarily, the Commission does not deal directly with any municipality or industry regarding compliance with its orders. It has won adherence to them through its educational efforts and by relying on the several pollution control agencies in the states. Not until 1957 did a situation arise that even suggested a need to use the Commission's enforcement powers. Even there, it was only necessary for the Commission to take the preliminary steps toward instituting enforcement procedures. As soon as it did so, the city of Gallipolis, to which the order had been issued, designed a program to bring the city into compliance with the Commission's requirements, and further enforcement action by the Commission has been withheld. The fact that it has not been necessary to rely on the enforcement power attests perhaps better than anything else to the

[24] The Interstate Sanitation Compact, in effect between New York and Connecticut, gives the Interstate Sanitation Commission power to bring action "in the proper court or courts to compel the enforcement of any and all of the provisions of [the] Compact" or of any of the Commission's orders made in pursuance thereof. (Article XI). No other Compact agencies are endowed with similar powers.

great power and prestige the Commission has built up in its ten-year career.

The Commission's activities are supported by pro rata appropriations from the party states, the amount each state contributes being set by a formula which takes into account the relative population and land area of that state in the Ohio River Basin. The Commission's budget is one of the largest among compact agencies. For some years it ran around $100,000 per annum and for 1955–1957 inclusive it was over $130,000. In addition to appropriations from the states, the Commission receives grants from the federal government under the terms of the Federal Water Pollution Control Act (Public Law 660), and a great deal of valuable voluntary assistance as well. Not only do the various industry action committees perform research for the Commission at no cost to the Commission, but much of the data on which the Commission bases its orders is contributed by industrial, municipal, state, and federal agencies. Were the actual cost of these services assumed by the Commission, its cost of operation might be as much as doubled.

The results of the Ohio River Valley Water Sanitation Commission's work have been impressive. Not long ago, a national magazine featured an article entitled "Rebirth of a Great River," a story about the new Ohio River, and the title does not overstate what the Commission has accomplished. In the words of the Commission's *9th Annual Summary* in 1957:

Today, more than three-quarters of the ten million sewered population of the valley is served by purification facilities in operation or being readied for operation as fast as construction contractors can complete them. In addition, another 11 percent of the population has final plans approved for a start on construction. By way of contrast . . . nine years ago [1948] less than 38 per cent of the population treated its sewage. The gain, percentagewise, in curbing pollution becomes even more impressive with the knowledge that there has been an increase of 1,600,000 people in the valley [during those nine years.][25]

When the Commission came into existence in 1948, less than one per cent of the population on the main stem of the Ohio River were served with adequate sewage treatment facilities; by 1957, adequate facilities were in operation or under construction to serve 86% of the valley's population. Of the more than 1200 communities in the basin, less than 300—and most of them very small towns—have not yet begun or completed adequate municipal sewage treatment plants. On the industrial side, the progress made under the aegis of the Commission has been almost as remarkable. In 1953, when accurate records first became available, out of 1247 industrial plants in the basin, only 323 had adequate pollution control facilities; by 1957, 717 out of 1431 plants had such facilities.[26] All told, more than two-thirds of the industrial plants discharging wastes into the streams of the basin now comply with the Commission's minimum requirements for pollution control.

The success of the Ohio River Valley Water Sanita-

[25] *9th Annual Summary*, 10.   [26] *Ibid.*, 5.

tion Commission can be attributed to a number of factors. For one thing, it has not deviated from the work prescribed by the Compact—pollution control. Although pollution is but one of many problems which exist in the Ohio River Basin, the Commission has steadfastly refused to be enticed by the possibilities of such problems as flood control, navigation, soil conservation, reforestation, and recreation. No doubt its way was made easier by the fact that all the party states already had an agency concerned wholly or in part with pollution control, with which the Commission could immediately begin to work and whose efforts it could begin to bring together into a massive attack. The Commission has always been respectful of these agencies, and in return the agencies have been willing to work with the Commission. The Commission's success on the industrial side can be credited in part to the dollars and cents value of stream sanitation which the Commission demonstrated in a great many cases. Finally, the Commission's success is due to its decision to rely mainly on education and persuasion to win adherence to its standards rather than on compulsion by law. Perhaps the most important result of its work is the creation of public awareness of and interest in attacking the pollution problem throughout the valley.

The Waterfront Commission of New York Harbor

The Waterfront Commission of New York Harbor is founded upon a compact between New York and New Jersey which went into effect December 1, 1953. It was the means finally adopted to eliminate notorious evils on the waterfront of New York's harbor which had been a public concern at least since 1916.[27] The immediate impetus was the investigation of conditions on the waterfront conducted by the New York State Crime Commission for Remedying Conditions on the Waterfront of the Port of New York. In its Fourth Report, the Crime Commission declared, "The evidence demonstrates that the Port of New York is in danger of losing the position of supremacy to which its natural advantages entitle it." Loss of the port's status would, the Commission felt, result in "a crushing blow to the prosperity of City and State." [28]

The status of the port was thus in danger because of corrupt and criminal practices in the steamship and stevedoring industry and in the related labor unions. The Commission's Report discusses such intolerable conditions as "the flagrant disregard by union officials of the welfare of their members," the habit of "corrupt labor leaders" of "engaging in incompatible business enterprises," vicious practices in the hiring of dock workers, the "ineffectiveness of the . . . pier watchman system," and the extortion practiced by "public loaders" who levied heavy fees on shippers for doing nothing. Accom-

[27] Exposés of the waterfront situation occur in the *Report on Dock Employment in New York City and Recommendations for its Regularization* (Mayor's Committee on Unemployment, 1916), the *Fourth Report of the New York State Crime Commission* (Leg. Doc. No. 70, 1953), the *Report of the New Jersey Law Enforcement Council* (1953), and the *Hearings Before Subcommittee of Committee on the Judiciary* (83rd Cong., 1st Sess., 1953).

[28] *Fourth Report of the New York State Crime Commission,* 7.

panying all this was a reign of terror marked by murder and mayhem.[29]

At the public hearings on the recommendations of the Crime Commission which Governor Thomas E. Dewey held June 8–9, 1953, nobody seriously disagreed with the findings of the Commission although representatives of the International Longshoremen's Association—the union under fire—protested its virtue. There was, however, uncertainty as to the most desirable means of remedying the situation. The City of New York, the states of New York and New Jersey singly or in concert, and the federal government were all suggested as the appropriate authority. The New York State Crime Commission had recommended the creation of a Division of Port Administration as "a separate division of one of the civil departments of the State of New York."[30] The difficulty with this was that the port is half in New York and half in New Jersey, but the waterfront must be treated as a whole. Parallel legislation by the two state legislatures was suggested, but participants in the hearings were quick to point out the administrative difficulties which would result. The city was ruled out on the grounds, first, of history, which indicated that it could not control the situation, and, again, of jurisdictional limitations. A bi-state approach was frequently advocated, most notably by Governor Dewey, but his idea was that the Port of New York Authority should assume the responsibility and the Authority did not wish to do so

The record of the hearings is instructive because in

[29] Cf. *ibid.*, 10.   [30] *Ibid.*, 68.

them one can see people gradually recognizing the necessity of interstate authority and moving, through the most diverse argument and testimony, toward sentiment for an interstate compact. Early in the hearings, Governor Dewey asked Austin J. Tobin, Director of the Port of New York Authority, to comment on the suggestion that the Port Authority "take on the job." Mr Tobin felt there would be a conflict of interest between the Port Authority's "general proprietary and financing" activities and the "type of state regulation and control that is talked of here." [31] At another point the possibility of federal regulation was broached and rejected because Congress could act only on conditions common to the ports of the country, and New York's were unique. Furthermore, it was pointed out, the Interstate Commerce Commission controls types of carriers which constituted a minor element in the Port of New York.[32] On the second day of the hearings, Governor Dewey remarked that "no one at yesterday's hearings proposed any feasible method of solving the problems we are meeting to discuss, except action by the State of New York or parallel action by [New York and] the State of New Jersey." And he repeated his reluctance to form a new division of state government. In response, Julius Hefland, Assistant District Attorney of Kings County, commented that it was the hope of his office "that if a bi-state commission could be organized, that that bi-state com-

[31] *Record of the Public Hearings . . . on the Recommendations of the New York State Crime Commission* (June 8 and 9, 1953), 15.
[32] *Ibid.,* 23.

mission be in the nature of the present Port Authority." [33]

Out of such interchanges came the Waterfront Commission Compact of 1953. Its opening article is a model
of explicitness about the motivating conditions and declares that the waterfront occupations "are affected with
a public interest requiring their regulation and that such
regulation shall be deemed an exercise of the police power
of the two states. . . ." [34] By its third article, the Compact creates the Waterfront Commission as a "body
corporate and politic, an instrumentality of the states of
New York and New Jersey." It consists of two members, one from New York and one from New Jersey, appointed by the governors with the advice of the senates
but without regard to state of residence. The Commissioners are to be compensated at a rate fixed by the governors and to be appointed for three-year terms. The
Commission acts by unanimous vote of both members. [35]

The Commission is endowed most explicitly with a
variety of powers. It is charged to administer and enforce the provisions of the Compact and given the means
to do so. It may "appoint such officers, agents and employees as it may deem necessary, prescribe their powers,
duties and qualifications and fix their compensation and
retain and employ counsel and private consultants on a
contract basis or otherwise." Furthermore, the Commission is given as distinct a place, administratively speaking,
in the families of the parent states as any other interstate

[33] *Ibid.*, 91–92.
[34] Waterfront Commission Compact, Article I.
[35] *Ibid.*, Article II.

compact agency. The Commission is required to make "annual and other reports to the governors and legislatures" stating its findings under several specified heads. More important, it is empowered "to cooperate with and receive from any department, division, bureau, board, commission, or agency of either or both states, or of any county or municipality thereof, such assistance and data as will enable it properly to carry out its powers and duties hereunder; and to request any such department . . . or agency, with the consent thereof, to execute such of its functions and powers, as the public interest may require." [36]

The first Commissioners were Lt. Gen. George P. Hays, for New York, and Maj. Gen. Edward C. Rose, for New Jersey. During the first year of its existence, the Commission completed its own organization, developed hearing procedures for the protection of the rights of individuals subject to its jurisdiction, and perfected licensing procedures designed to regulate the longshoremen's occupation. The Commission audited the books and records of stevedoring corporations and began the licensing of port watchmen, checking them, like the longshoremen, for criminal records and activities and for physical and mental fitness. In accordance with the Compact, the Commission eliminated public loading and caused the work to be done by the steamship lines and stevedoring corporations with registered longshoremen. The Commission established thirteen employment information centers through which all longshoremen except those who worked regularly and almost exclusively for a

[36] *Ibid.*, Article IV.

single employer were hired, a procedure designed to replace the notorious "shape-up" system which the Crime
Commission had strenuously condemned. Meanwhile
the investigative staff of the Commission was developing
"an increasing amount of information regarding illegal
waterfront activities" and cooperating with other agencies in the complex task of controlling "leaders of criminal activities on the waterfront who are beyond the
jurisdiction of the Waterfront Commission because they
do not work as longshoremen or hiring agents or in other
licensed occupations." [37]

In succeeding years, the Commission continued its
work in the areas mentioned and gradually shifted emphasis from the licensing of waterfront workers to the
enforcement of its regulations and to the investigation of
the persistent criminal and quasi-criminal activities which
formerly thrived unimpeded at the port. As it matured,
the Commission reorganized its staff and adopted a
systematic salary plan for its personnel. The Commission's Executive Director served also, in the beginning, as
General Counsel, but this arrangement was altered in
November, 1955, and replaced by two distinct and coordinate positions. By April, 1956, it was apparent that
the new arrangement was inefficient, so the Commission
revised its by-laws again, making the Executive Director
"generally in administrative charge of all Commission
personnel and all Commission activities." [38] Also in
1956, the Commission made a salary survey of its per-

[37] Waterfront Commission of New York Harbor, *Annual Report 1953–54*, pp. 1–3.
[38] *Idem, Annual Report 1955–56*, p. 3.

sonnel in comparison with those of other government agencies and private employers. It then established fourteen salary grades with minimum, intermediate, and maximum compensation in each grade. In accordance with job analyses, employees were placed in appropriate grades. Increments are granted upon certification by division heads that employees have performed competently.[39] By 1956, the Commission was calling for additional personnel to devote to the enforcement phases of its work. The 1956–57 budget provided for additional attorneys and investigators, but even so the largest unit of the Commission's employees work in the employment information centers.

The Commission has four operating divisions: the Division of Law and Enforcement, the Division of Employment Information Centers and Licensing, the Division of Investigation, and the Division of Administration. The director of each division selects his employees with the approval of the Executive Director and the Commission. Since the establishment of the salary grade plan in 1956, personnel policies have been further defined. Merit raises are allowed. The Commission established a policy of promoting from within wherever possible at the time of its formation, but its employees are not under Civil Service and they do not have tenure. They enjoy the full range of "fringe benefits"—Social Security, group hospitalization, sick leave, vacations, and group life insurance.

The Waterfront Commission derives its revenues from an assessment upon the payrolls of registered and licensed employees of stevedores, steamship companies, and

[39] *Ibid.*, 4.

watching agencies. The levy, fixed by statute at a maximum of two per cent, is collected quarterly. New York and New Jersey advanced the Commission $900,000 to begin operations, and by the end of 1956 fiscal year this amount had been repaid. The Commission's budget exceeded two million dollars in 1958.

Within less than three years, the Waterfront Commission had essentially solved the problems which had plagued the New York waterfront for half a century. Obviously, the specifically interstate authority which it represents was necessary to handle the situation. Competing jurisdictions within each of the states concerned made impossible the "parallel" action which was often recommended. Only by unifying the authority for regulation of the waterfront could the end be achieved. The dramatic reduction of crime and violence on the waterfront and the increase in the prosperity and good name of the Port of New York since the Commission was formed are the evidence that support the proposition that an interstate compact was the required specific. The Compact requires the Commission to state in its annual reports whether public necessity still exists for the continued registration of longshoremen, the continued licensing of any occupation or employment required to be licensed under the Compact, and the continued public operation of the employment information centers. There is no reason to expect that the Commission will ever be able in conscience to report negatively, for no other means than the interstate compact is available to govern the interstate waterfront.

The Interstate Oil Compact Commission

The Interstate Oil Compact was a direct result of the glut in oil production which followed the discovery and development of the vast new oil fields in Texas and Oklahoma between 1925 and 1930. Neither state had adequate control laws, and some sort of federal conservation program seemed inevitable to prevent complete demoralization of the oil industry. However, resistance to federal intervention—to "federal encroachment on state sovereignty," in the words of a later chairman of the Interstate Oil Compact Commission,[40]—was strong, and under the leadership of the then governor of Oklahoma, E. W. Marland, an agreement was reached among the major oil producing states—Colorado, Illinois, Kansas, New Mexico, Oklahoma, and Texas—to handle the problem through an interstate compact. The Interstate Compact to Conserve Oil and Gas was drafted early in 1935. It was approved by Congress and became effective that same year. Since then, twenty-three other states and territories have approved the Compact, and Congress has repeatedly renewed its consent, most recently for the four-year period ending September 1, 1959.

While the Interstate Oil Compact was drafted primarily to forestall federal action in regard to conservation, there was no desire among its framers to entrust conservation to a powerful interstate agency either. It has always been emphasized that the Compact was merely

[40] Johnston Murray, "From Anarchy to State Agreement," *The Interstate Oil Compact Quarterly Bulletin*, XI (September, 1952), 13.

a "restatement of the rights of the Sovereign States to each run their own affairs." [41] Thus the Interstate Oil Compact Commission was not made a regulatory agency, with power to set allowable production limits and to impose a general pattern of conservation legislation on the party states. Instead, it was established solely as "an exchange table for views on waste prevention" [42] and endowed with recommendatory power only. The Compact made it perfectly clear that while the states might act independently of the Commission, the Commission was not free to act without the approval of the states. Thus Article III declares that "the scope of the authority of any state" over conservation shall in no way be limited by acts of the Commission. Even more significantly, Article VII provides that no state by joining the Compact shall become financially obligated in any way as a result.

Because the states were so obviously concerned to protect their own sovereignty and to limit the power of the Commission, early estimates of the Commission's effectiveness were all pessimistic. It was widely felt that the Compact contained no "genuinely effective terms" and that it "was entered into by the States which signed it with full knowledge that it did not do anything." [43] Such judgments, however, failed to take into account the real heart of the Compact, as far as the Commission is

[41] E. O. Thompson, "Fifteen Years of Accomplishments of the Interstate Oil Compact Commission," *The Interstate Oil Compact Quarterly Bulletin*, IX (December, 1950), 10.

[42] E. O. Thompson to Richard H. Leach, August 10, 1956.

[43] Remarks of Charles A. Wolverton, Representative from New Jersey, in debate, U.S. House of Representatives, August 24, 1935, 79 *Congressional Record*, 14591.

concerned, which is Article IV. It directs the Commission to study "methods, practices, circumstances, and conditions. . . . for bringing about conservation and the prevention of physical waste of oil and gas" and to report "at such intervals as said Commission deems beneficial . . . its findings and recommendations to the several states for adoption or rejection." The Commission is thus given a twofold job: to discover and develop new methods and practices of conservation and to promote their adoption and use by the states. It is both a fact-finding and a promotional body. Its power lies in the quality of its recommendations and its ability to persuade the states to accept them.

Lacking the power to coerce, the Commission has had to make the most of the only power it does possess, the power to persuade. This has required involving the "right" people in each member state in the Commission's activities and thus making up in prestige what it lacks in power. Fortunately, the Commission itself, which consists of one representative from each state, includes the governors of the party states. A governor is traditionally chosen chairman of the Commission, and collectively the governors play a leading role in Commission activities. Almost without exception, they have assumed responsibility for urging acceptance of recommendations by the Commission before their respective legislatures. The Commission's recommendations have never been very hard to sell because it was early decided to leave their framing to experts in all phases of conservation—to scientists, lawyers, engineers, geologists—who form the half dozen standing committees of the Commission. A small Commission staff assists the committees in their work, but it is generally acknowledged that the committees, the members of which are not ordinarily members of the Commission, constitute the real working end of the Commission. It does not exaggerate their importance to say that their studies and reports for the Commission have had more impact on oil and gas conservation practices in the United States than those from any other quarter.

The Commission concerns itself not only with the study and recommendation of more effective methods of oil and gas conservation, but also with an extensive campaign to educate the public about conservation. "The Interstate Oil Compact Commission," noted one of its former chairmen, "considers an enlightened public opinion to be the greatest support of good conservation programs. When the public realizes its dependence on and its benefits from oil and gas, sound conservation practices and laws will follow." [44] To this end, it engages in a large-scale publications program. The Commission also serves as the watchdog of the oil-producing states in Congress and before the federal regulatory agencies, both through resolutions passed at Commission meetings and forwarded to the proper federal agencies and through the lobbying of individual Commission members and members of the Commission staff in Washington. Members of the Commission and of the staff also are frequently

[44] Governor Johnston Murray of Oklahoma, in a mimeographed release of the Interstate Oil Compact Commission dated July 22, 1954, accompanying copies of the pamphlet "What Oil Conservation Means to You."

invited to appear before state legislative committees, Congressional committees, and federal regulatory agencies to testify on various phases of oil and gas conservation.

They attend most of the oil and gas association meetings as well as the meetings of many technical and professional organizations with an interest in oil and gas in an advisory capacity and provide liaison between those groups and the Commission. Finally, the Commission provides through its meetings a forum for the exchange of information on all aspects of the petroleum industry. All Commission meetings are open, and an earnest effort is made to answer every question asked. As a result, Commission meetings are teaching sessions where participants learn of new processes, are advised of new techniques, become acquainted with developments in other states, and contribute to each other's understanding and knowledge of effective conservation practices. Since Commission proceedings are published, the same information is also available to a far greater audience. During the last few years, the Commission has undertaken to enlarge its library and to make it "a clearing house for information on oil and gas conservation of national and perhaps international importance . . . able to furnish any person interested in this material the location of any publication or subject matter that he may desire." [45] Within a few years this function may become one of the Commission's important activities.

Commission operations are financed entirely by volun-

[45] *The Interstate Oil Compact Quarterly Bulletin*, XIV (June, 1955), 149.

tary contributions from member and associate states. No other contributions are accepted. Recent budgets have been in the vicinity of $100,000 per annum. The member states have been meticulous about supporting the Commission and have generally kept their contributions adjusted to inflation and the rising cost of living. As might be expected, Oklahoma and Texas are the largest contributors. The bulk of each year's budget goes for staff salaries, committee expenses and travel, and printing and library expenses.

Perhaps no compact commission in the United States has so effectively accomplished its objective and been so consistently popular while doing so as the Interstate Oil Compact Commission. "There is no doubt," one observer has commented, "but that the Commission could halt any type of [oil or gas] waste in the United States by holding a hearing, the determination of that waste by the Commission, and a publication of its findings." [46] Under its leadership, the states have developed an eminently satisfactory framework of conservation law. So direct is the Commission's role that the suggested form of oil and gas conservation laws prepared by the Commission's Legal Committee has been the basis for virtually all development in state conservation law since 1935. Moreover, the Commission has done a great deal to advance methods for increasing ultimate recovery of oil and gas. The need for federal action in the field has been completely obviated.

It must be recogized, however, that the Commission

[46] Blakely M. Murphy, *Conservation of Oil and Gas, A Legal History* (Chicago, 1949), 577.

has been successful partly because of the passage of the so-called "Connally Hot Oil Act" [47] which supports state conservation laws by prohibiting the shipment in interstate commerce of oil produced in excess of that allowed by state regulatory agencies. In all its actions, however, the Commission has won the unanimous praise of the member states, of the federal government, and of the oil industry itself.

The Southern Regional Education Board

Of all the interstate compact agencies, the Southern Regional Education Board is the most complex in conception and in operation. It presents some features of the public authority-type and of the technical type although its advisory and research functions are sufficiently stressed to associate it primarily with the study-recommendatory type of compact agency. Established in 1949, it was the model for the Western Interstate Commission on Higher Education (1953) and the New England Board of Higher Education (1955). Its complexity reflects that of higher education, both as to subject matter and as to administration. Although established to handle what were thought of as peculiarly Southern problems, the Board rapidly proved that the interstate compact approach to higher education had intrinsic merit as its adoption outside the South testifies.

The Southern Regional Education Compact has been ratified by sixteen states including Oklahoma and Texas and all the states east and south of the Ohio River. The program touches some thirty fields of graduate and pro-

[47] 49 Stat. 30 (1935).

fessional education, involves in varying degree some sixty-five universities, directly affects about a thousand students every year, and represents the expenditure of about $1,500,000 annually from state funds, not to mention varying amounts in grants from private foundations and federal government agencies. The Board employs a professional staff located in Atlanta.

The Compact opens with the announcement that the states concerned have been considering "the establishment and maintenance of jointly owned and operated regional education institutions . . . in the professional, technological, scientific, literary, and other fields." It mentions that Meharry Medical College (Nashville) has proposed that the Southern states jointly operate it, and that the states do wish to enter into a compact "providing for the planning and establishment of regional education facilities." These are the only reasons given to explain why the states concluded to "form a geographical district or region consisting of the area lying within the boundaries of the contracting states which, for the purposes of this compact, shall constitute an area for regional education supported by public funds derived from taxation . . . and . . . from other sources for the establishment, acquisition, operation and maintenance of regional educational schools and institutions for the benefit of citizens of the respective states."

Proponents of the use of compacts in higher education have often regretted the plain reference to Meharry Medical College, a Negro institution which was in financial straits in spite of the great shortage of facilities for training doctors and dentists that existed in the South at the time the Compact was written. The significance of Meharry is further suggested by the fact that it was preparing approximately half of the nation's Negro graduates in medicine and dentistry. Meharry was saved by the "contracts for services" which the Board worked out as the first means of implementing the Compact. If Meharry alone had profited, the Board might still be accused of having set out only to preserve a Negro institution in order to make segregation practicable. The fact is that of the eighteen to twenty institutions which have contracted through the Board to accept students from states lacking facilities in medical, veterinary, dental, or social-work education, only three are primarily for Negroes. Of the roughly one thousand "regional students" enrolled in any given year, about one-fourth are Negroes. The inference is that the Board addressed itself to problems of higher education as such regardless of race.

It was no less important during the first years to establish cordial relations with Southern colleges and universities than to avoid identification with the race issue. For here lay the crucial question whether the Board could create a positive program. The Compact provides that the Board may establish and operate regional institutions, and many institutions were apprehensive of competition from this quarter. The Board adopted by-laws at its organizational meeting which included a policy of working only with existing, accredited colleges and universities insofar as possible. This left it in the situation of having to work largely by persuasion and with the entirely voluntary cooperation of the universities although it never relinquished any authority. Nevertheless, it was feared that the Board would designate "centers of distinction" in various fields among the universities of the region. Was the Board then to become a powerful sort of accrediting—in the sense of pace-setting—agency allied directly with the governors and legislatures of its constituent states?

The Compact raised such questions in the minds of many but specified no program. Rather, it created the Board and charged it to do so. Board membership was to include the governors of the participating states, *ex officio*, and three persons appointed by each; the only restriction was that one must be an educator. Since then, the representation of each state has been increased to five, the fifth member being a legislator. The typical group from a state includes, by custom, administrators of colleges and universities in addition to the political figures. So constituted, the Board proceeded at once to state in its by-laws that its purpose was to assist states, institutions, and agencies concerned with higher education "to advance knowledge and improve the social and economic level of the Southern region." In doing this, it would serve as a clearinghouse for information of regional significance about higher education; provide continuous assessment of the needs of higher education in the region and make plans to meet them; administer interstate arrangements for educational services; and develop research and consultation services relating to higher education.

Instead of acting on the authority to found institutions which the Compact grants but which experience indicated would kill the program, the Board set about winning support for the concept of interstate cooperation. During the first two years, it conducted a series of conferences and studies involving hundreds of college and university personnel, state officials, and representatives of the professions and industry. The contracts for services already mentioned and "Memoranda of Agreement" were the Board's first concrete answers to the fears that it would set up new institutions or dictate to existing ones.

By means of the contracts, states engage with the Board to find places for quotas of their residents in accredited schools, and the Board in turn contracts with institutions to accept the "regional students." The Board also receives agreed-upon sums of money per student from the state and disburses them to the schools. Thus the Board serves as administrative agency and buffer so effectively that private universities, jealous of their independence from government influence, participate as readily in the contract programs as state institutions. Until the foundation of its own medical school, Florida, for example, subsidized the medical education of scores of students at the medical schools of Emory and Duke Universities. A "regional school," as developed through the contracts, is simply one which is supported by a number of states instead of by a single state. The School of Veterinary Medicine at the Alabama Polytechnic Institute, for instance, has contracts with Florida, Kentucky, Mississippi, and Tennessee, and serves those states precisely as it serves Alabama. The contracting states are thus relieved of the expense of establishing veterinary schools while the Alabama school gains needed supplements for its budget.

The Memoranda of Agreement, on the other hand, are documents which declare the intention of universities with accredited schools or departments in given fields to co-operate in making available to the region a jointly planned program based on objective study of the region's needs. The schools remain independent but undertake to offer a complementary series instead of a number of wastefully competitive programs. An impressive achievement under a Memorandum of Agreement is the program of graduate education in nursing involving Emory University, the Universities of Alabama, Maryland, North Carolina and Texas, and Vanderbilt University. The schools of nursing at these universities are cooperating with each other and with the Southern Regional Education Board in offering curriculums leading to the master's degree for nursing supervisors, administrators, instructors, and psychiatric nurses. Formerly the South offered graduate work only in public health nursing. Grants from two foundations enabled the schools to begin their programs in 1954 and 1955. The regional or interstate character of the undertaking depends on a "regional committee" consisting of the nursing school deans and a Board staff member. This committee conducts a seminar attended by the deans and, from time to time, members of the faculties of the cooperating schools. The seminar plans, coordinates, and evaluates the several programs, and the regional committee allocates fellowship funds.

From such studies as that from which the nursing program evolved, the Board has gradually undertaken more general research on problems of higher education. The most substantial accomplishments to date have been projections of college enrollment in the several states of the Compact; the surveys which preceded the establishment of the Southern Regional Council on Mental Health Training and Research; and a catalogue of doctoral programs offered by Southern universities. The results are published as aids to states and universities in planning their activities within the regional context and, independently of given projects, simply as contributions to the subjects concerned. The Board strongly advocates state-wide studies of higher education and provides consultation for them by members of its staff. The Board's interest stems from the fact that interstate action depends in the end on the rationalization of higher education within the constituent states; for until states are clear as to their purposes and needs, they find it difficult to determine the regional services which they should either give or receive.

The Board's interest in research on the general problems of higher education received new impetus in 1957 from a grant by the Carnegie Corporation of New York. The Board emphasizes the stimulation of research at colleges and universities of the South rather than by its own staff on such subjects as admissions policies and the financing of higher education. At present, it is engaged in cooperative projects with the University of Maryland, dealing with motivations for college teaching, and with the University of Kentucky, dealing with graduate pro-

208

grams to prepare college teachers. In addition, the Board provides four research fellowships annually for persons who wish to work on problems of higher education and who will probably continue or apply such study at some institutions in the South.

As the Southern Regional Education Compact requires, the Board is supported primarily by appropriations from the constituent states although it is authorized to accept funds from other sources too. Each state is currently appropriating $20,000 annually to the Board. The subsidies of education under the contracts for services are made in addition to the appropriations for support of the Board and its staff. The latter is headed by a director and organized, at this writing, into sections devoted to the development and administration of "regional programs"—the activities under the contracts and memoranda of agreement, for example; to the development and coordination of research and training in several mental health fields at Southern universities; and to research on higher education as indicated above.

No account of the program being carried out under the Southern Regional Education Compact would be adequate without reference to the numerous groups which work either within the organization developed by the Board or in relation to it. The Board's intimate relation to the Southern Governors' Conference is of primary importance. The governors adopted the regional education movement as one of their first major projects, and their *ex officio* membership on the Board has resulted in the annual meeting of the Board being held in conjunction with the Southern Governors' Conference. This group tends increasingly to use the Board as a research and advisory agency in matters not directly concerned with higher education. It did so in 1953, for example, when it requested the Board to make the surveys of mental health training and research which have been mentioned and to recommend interstate action to alleviate the states' problems in obtaining sufficient personnel for their mental health programs. Again, in 1955, it put the Board into a new role by asking it to organize a regional conference on the potential uses of nuclear power in Southern commerce and industry and their implications for education and the professions.[48]

Scarcely less significant than the relation to the governors is the Board's legislative connection. Since 1952 the Board has conducted an annual Legislative Work Conference on Southern Regional Education to which the governors appoint delegations of key legislators. This Work Conference has become an interstate forum in which the problems and possibilities of advanced education are discussed by the men who so largely control its budget.[49]

From the beginning, the Southern Regional Education Board has had to win support from diverse groups—ranging from college administrators and faculties to legislators and industrialists—by involving them in the planning of its projects. It has had to allay suspicion, especially among the universities themselves, that it would

[48] For an account of this activity, see Redding S. Sugg, Jr. (ed.), *Nuclear Energy in the South* (Baton Rouge, 1957).

[49] Reports of the Legislative Work Conference are available from the office of the Board.

seek to dominate higher education throughout the immense region covered by the Compact. And yet, as the Board concludes its tenth year of operation, it seems to have made a permanent place for itself. Out of the experimental variety of activities which it has undertaken, a number which have proven particularly susceptible to an interstate or an inter-institutional approach are being emphasized. The interstate compact programs in higher education being developed in the West and in New England both reflect and refine the Southern experience, clearly suggesting the practicability of the interstate compact as a device for attacking very general and even abstract problems as well as the administratively limited, technical ones first considered in this chapter.

6: Some Conclusions and Predictions

The record shows that all of the compact agencies have made significant contributions toward the solution of the problems they were designed to meet. Thanks to compact agencies, great ports are being competently managed; oil is being conserved more effectively than ever before; higher education in the South, in New England, and throughout the West is being strengthened in a variety of ways; the pollution of streams is being reduced in great river basins; parks are being built and maintained; the difficulties of metropolitan transportation are being approached intelligently; water is being apportioned fairly and water resources developed in numerous river systems; research is being carried on in a variety of fields relating to fisheries which were formerly entirely neglected; and crime in the neighborhood of the Port of New York is at last being controlled. Even the Delaware River Joint Toll Bridge Commission, the only compact agency which has been touched by scandal, is accomplishing its objectives, clearing in tolls for 1957 $3,361,-

742—a sum which emphasizes both its effectiveness and the weight of its responsibilities.

The interstate compact agencies have succeeded for a number of definable reasons. First, no doubt, is the high quality of their work. An important reason for this is the fact that none of them has tried to do too much. This effective focus is a tribute to the framers of the compacts, which typically define the scope of the agencies they create in clear terms.

Another condition of success has been the circumstance that all of the agencies now operating were created by the states in the realization that the best and, in some instances, the only way to handle the issues in question was to establish a compact agency to do the job. Each interstate compact agency has been problem-oriented from the start, growing from a particular situation the logic of which made for a favorable atmosphere. Moreover, no compact agency has in any sense been imposed upon a state, and none has been assigned powers which threatened existing powers within the states. With regard to some compact agencies, fears were expressed at first that they would usurp the prerogatives of existing state agencies and might even be in a position to dominate them. In practice, every compact agency has been careful to avoid even the appearance of such ambition.

The effectiveness of the compact agencies may be further explained by the fact that every one of them has enjoyed the support and the services of a small group of dedicated men—appointed members and staff. Their good fortune in enlisting competent personnel may be explained, in turn, by the observation that they are effective as units of administration. They are small enough to be flexible in action and to develop the personal enthusiasm of their members and staff. Not being bound by precedent, they can experiment with greater freedom than most governmental units.

The compact agencies doubtless owe their success in part also to the support they have received from the Council of State Governments, from many of the state Commissions on Interstate Cooperation, and from various branches of the federal government. The latter, of course, have underwritten some compact programs. The U.S. Geological Survey and the U.S. Public Health Service, to mention only two federal agencies, have played key roles in the operations of the compact agencies concerned with water allocation and pollution control.

As the record grows, it becomes apparent that perhaps the most important element in the success of the interstate compact agencies has been their contentment with the status of decidedly state instrumentalities. That is, they have never attempted to alter the federal system or developed a doctrinaire attitude. With so many compact agencies in operation, one might expect to find them pushing to replace the traditional two-level concept of federalism with a three-level one making room for what might be called "interstatism." No longer, they might be expected to argue, need the American people be limited to governmental services by the federal government on the one hand and the states on the other; for a third force, constituted by the compact agencies, is available to mitigate the shortcomings of the old system.

Some Conclusions and Predictions

So firmly did Felix Frankfurter and James M. Landis hold this point of view when they wrote their pioneering study of interstate compacts that they described the development of a new "regionalism" in the United States. Nothing was clearer to them "than that in the United States there [were] being built up regional interests, regional cultures, and regional interdependencies. These produce regional problems calling for regional solutions. Control by the nation . . . would be ill-conceived and intrusive. . . . [Instead] regional interests, regional wisdom and regional pride must be looked to for solutions. . . . Collective legislative action through the instrumentality of Compacts by states constituting a region [furnished the answer]." They declared further, "The overwhelming difficulties confronting modern society must not be at the mercy of the false antithesis embodied in the shibboleths 'States-Rights' and 'National Supremacy.' " [1] Interstate compacts provided the middle way, the way of regional action.

Far from supporting this forecast, the record of the interstate compact agencies calls into doubt even the more restrained view, expressed by George C. S. Benson and Marshall Dimock, that a compact agency might "well be the alternative to action by impotent, devitalized states on the one hand and [by] an overburdened national government on the other." [2] Instead, the compact agencies, especially those created since World War

[1] Frankfurter and Landis, "The Compact Clause of the Constitution—A Study in Interstate Adjustments," *loc. cit.*, 707–708, 729.

[2] Dimock and Benson, *Can Interstate Compacts Succeed?*, 21.

II, must be regarded as the carefully selected tools of energetic states anxious to exert their powers effectively. They have been created in an atmosphere of confidence and in the expectation that through them the people of the party states would be satisfactorily served.

Despite the fact that most of the compacts set up a geographical district (which might be thought of as a region in the sense used by Frankfurter and Landis), within which the agencies are authorized to operate, the party states have not regarded the compact agencies as regional units distinct from themselves. They plainly regard them as instrumentalities of state power which enable the states to work together in reaching particular goals. The states have made it clear from the beginning that they like the prospect of independently powerful interstate authority as little as they like the possibility of still greater federal control. Their concern has been to protect their own power from both the compact agencies and the federal government, and they have done this by using compacts to create agencies for joint *state* action rather than for regional action philosophically conceived. Had the compact agencies gone against this sentiment in any fashion they would hardly have survived, much less grown in popularity.

Regardless of their success in given activities, the interstate compact agencies may be considered in the light of the question whether they have "measured up to expectations held for them when they were created." [3] The

[3] Emil J. Sady, *Research in Federal-State Relations: A Report on Recent Developments and Problems Requiring Further Study* (Washington, D.C., 1957), 47.

answer is more difficult to formulate than the question to frame. In the first place, it is not always easy to ascertain what expectations were held for a compact agency when it was created. The framers of the Interstate Oil Compact, for example, were evidently much more concerned to prevent federal encroachment on state sovereignty than they were to facilitate interstate cooperation to conserve oil. Throughout its history, the Compact has been regarded primarily as an exercise of the right of the signatory states to handle conservation as they saw fit. A strong compact commission was the furthest thing from their minds.[4] Viewed against this background, the accomplishments of the Interstate Oil Compact Commission are even more impressive. Similarly, the framers of the Southern Regional Education Compact probably did not expect that the Southern Regional Education Board would develop as it has. There is much to indicate that they thought the Board would play a much greater role in helping the Southern states adjust to changes in the racial situation. They certainly had no inkling of the contracts, Memoranda of Agreement, and other means the Board has developed to organize interstate support for programs of higher education.

Even where it is clear what the expectations of the framers of a compact were, it may be misleading to judge the agency's record accordingly. In more than one instance, the expectations were misguided. To say that the compact agency lived up to expectations in such a situation would be to condemn it. The Ohio River Valley Water Sanitation Compact is a case in point. It seems

[4] See 79 *Congressional Record* (1935), 14591.

to have been framed with the expectation that the Commission would be an enforcement agency, using its power under the Compact to secure compliance through the courts. The Commission has, however, avoided the use of that power altogether and with good reason: its record of accomplishment has been better without it. Yet if judged in terms of the expectations of the men who framed the Compact, it could easily be called a failure.

Again, the expectations of the framers of some compacts have been wholly unrealistic. A great deal is made of the fact that the Rio Grande Compact Commission, for example, has not brought peace to the Texas-New Mexico water front, despite its objective, prescribed in the Compact, to improve interstate comity. Judged in terms of the rest of the Compact, however, the Rio Grande Commission has been a success. The cogent comment may be simply that the states not having composed their controversy, the compact agency should hardly be expected to do it.

The interstate compact, abstractly considered, has on occasion been judged for *not* meeting certain problems. Thus Harvey Mansfield argues that "it is prudent to look at Compact failures, and these abound in the watershed development field" and remarks that the only successful examples of unified basin development have been the work of the national government.[5] But no interstate compacts have yet been framed to unify watershed devel-

[5] Harvey C. Mansfield, "The States in the American System," ch. 1 of *The Forty-Eight States: Their Tasks as Policy Makers and Administrators,* "A Report of the American Assembly" (New York, 1955), 34.

opment, and no compact agencies have undertaken such work. Thus there have been no compact failures in this area because there have been no compacts. And it would be unfair to assert that a compact agency could not do what a federal agency has done and do it as well, given a chance. Nothing in the procedures or principles of compact agency operation automatically prevents an interstate compact agency from performing as satisfactorily as any other type of governmental unit.

With all these caveats entered, the question still remains: Have compact agencies lived up to the expectations held for them when they were created? The answer in general is yes. A clear affirmative can be given for such venerable agencies as the Port of New York Authority, the Interstate Oil Compact Commission, the Atlantic States Marine Fisheries Commission, and the Interstate Sanitation Commission because they have been in operation long enough to see their accomplishments in perspective. Naturally, a less positive answer must be given with respect to the newer agencies. On the other hand, none of this group has definitely failed. Since the states continue to support every agency now in operation, it may be assumed that all of them are succeeding to some extent. No party state has refused to support a compact agency in operation; rather, when it has been necessary to increase their appropriations, the party states have done so. This continued support indicates better than anything else that the states are satisfied with what they have created.

Perhaps a more significant basis of judgment would be the question: Are compact agencies meeting the current problems in their respective fields? For most of them, the answer is again affirmative. Of course, some of them are prevented from doing so by one or more terms of the compact under which they operate. The Interstate Commission for the Potomac River Basin, for example, is seriously handicapped by a $30,000 budget ceiling in the Compact itself, and the southwestern water allocation commissions are precluded from moving in the important direction of water-resources development by the narrowness of the compacts on which they are founded. Generally, within the framework of the compacts under which they work, interstate compact agencies have shown imagination and enterprise in seeking out and meeting problems within their area of interest. It is significant in this regard to point out the frequent self-analyses many agencies subject themselves to: the Southern Regional Education Board, for instance, has from the beginning almost continuously examined its own procedures and assessed its ability to define and select appropriate problems of higher education in the South for attack; the Interstate Sanitation Commission likewise has continually surveyed the area of its concern to see if it is giving the greatest service it can. Its recent assumption of the responsibility for a study of the problems of air pollution in the tri-state district in which it operates is a good example of the seriousness with which it approaches its opportunities. The Interstate Oil Compact Commission's recent appointment of a standing committee to study the effect of oil imports on domestic conservation programs is still another example of the initiative of compact agencies in addressing themselves to new problems in their fields.

More searching, however, than either of the questions asked is the further question: Are the compact agencies making the greatest possible contribution to the solution of American governmental problems? In part the answer lies hidden in the future. Compact agencies have been extensively employed only since World War II. It takes time to develop the habit of using any new social tool, and even more time to fit its use into the already complicated pattern of American federalism. If at present compact agencies are not making as great a contribution as they might, time alone can probably be counted on to increase the role they will play in American life. In part the answer lies in the degree to which the states accept compact agencies as extensions of themselves to act in areas where states are individually ineffectual. Although compact agencies are being created more frequently now than ever before, their total number is still very small; and, when the total of all the people involved in compact agency operations—commission members and staff —in the United States today is compared to the numbers employed in a single federal bureau or a department of one of the larger states, the relative position of compact agencies in the American governmental picture may be clearly grasped. Although the areas covered by compact today are far more numerous than they were a generation ago, and the compacts themselves more imaginative, compacts and compact agencies taken as a whole must be recognized as very junior members of the American governmental family. Although it has been predicted that compact agencies will become "a major device for the administration of multi-state facilities and functions," [6] they have not yet achieved that status.

Interstate compact agencies will probably not be more freely used until they are more widely known and understood not only by legislators, state executive officers, and governors, but also by the public. A concentrated drive to publicize the accomplishments and possibilities of compact agencies would accomplish part of the job, and most agencies themselves in their public relations and information activities have made commendable beginnings in that direction. More is needed, however. A considerable hostility toward compact agencies exists because of a number of charges which have been raised against them over the years. In every state the same charges are leveled and it is time they were exposed as baseless.

For example, the charge that compact agencies are peculiarly irresponsible, beyond the reach of the people when once set up, falls flat upon examination. For the same is true of the Department of Motor Vehicles of the State of Kansas, of the Passport Division of the U.S. Department of State, of the Senate Committee on Non-Essential Expenditures, of the United States Supreme Court, and of many other agencies which are without strong external checks. The significant question is whether an adequate internal, subjective sense of responsibility—of dedication to the public welfare—has developed in the members of compact agencies generally and in their staffs

[6] Zimmermann and Wendell, *The Interstate Compact Since 1925*, p. 2.

so as to make external checks unnecessary. And this question must be answered affirmatively. Probably no more responsible group of public officials exists in the United States than those associated with compact agencies. The members are generally competent and do a conscientious job, and the stability and performance record of the average compact agency staff testify to high quality.

A second criticism of compact agencies has been that they are staff dominated and thus all the more irresponsible. It is true, as has been shown, that in virtually every case, the commission, board, or authority created by compact is composed of persons whose main interests and chief responsibilities lie elsewhere, so that implementation of the compacts and direction of staff can at best be but secondary concerns to them. It is equally true that most compact agencies come to be identified in the public mind and in legislative circles with their staffs and not with the members themselves. The typical staff, under its executive director, tends both to initiate and to carry out policy.

No doubt under certain circumstances such a situation could lead to irresponsibility, but the same practice is common among boards of many state and federal agencies and reaches into the White House itself. Indeed, the practice is common outside of government as well—university faculties usually complain if it is otherwise with their trustees and many a business would falter if total responsibility were left with the board of directors. The charge against compact agencies does not stand up under examination because their staffs, like those of state departments, federal bureaus, universities, and industrial concerns, are generally men of probity who have a sense of dedication to the job. They are responsible in fact if not in theory. The record indicates the existence of close and harmonious relations between compact commissions and their staffs, which have resulted in responsibly directed action toward the accomplishment of the objectives of the several compacts.

A third charge sometimes made against compact agencies is that it is hard to tell when they are doing a good job because as yet no adequate way of judging the effectiveness of compact operation has been evolved. Thus, critics allege, compact agencies, once launched, and left as they are to exist in a twilight zone of public consciousness, may never accomplish what they might or should. As a consequence, they may become less concerned with performance than with successful public relations—with winning approval by word instead of deed. This, however, is a difficulty which is present across the board in governmental operation and can be charged no more against compact agencies than against any other form of governmental agency. Evaluation of program accomplishment generally is still a virgin territory, unconquered either by theorists or by practitioners in public administration. The interstate compact agencies may not, therefore, be specially cited for not having developed evaluative procedures.

Interstate compact agencies have proved themselves by their performance and, more than that, they have demonstrated the utility of the interstate compact as an instrument of state policy. In the years just ahead, the states will no doubt make even more use of that device than they have to date. President Eisenhower has been concerned from the beginning of his first administration to restore power to the states and to prevent them from degenerating "into powerless satellites of the National Government in Washington." [7] From all sides he has received support. The Kestnbaum Commission devoted considerable attention to strengthening state government and to developing "the capacity of the States to handle a larger share of the total task of government" in the United States.[8] The Eighth American Assembly of the Graduate School of Business of Columbia University devoted itself to the question of the tasks of the states as policy makers and administrators and concluded that "strengthening of our state governments is imperative. The states must accept promptly their changing responsibilities if they are to continue to be strong and vital parts of our federal system." [9] The U.S. Chamber of Commerce has recognized the same problem and come to the same conclusion.[10] The nineteen-fifties have produced in the United States renewed emphasis on the position and powers of the states in the federal union.

As the states accept the challenge, they will need every

[7] Address at the State Dinner of the 1957 Governors' Conference, Williamsburg, Virginia, June 24, 1957.

[8] The Commission on Intergovernmental Relations, *A Report to the President for Transmittal to the Congress*, June, 1955, p. 37.

[9] Mansfield, "The States in the American System," *loc. cit.*, 138.

[10] See Chamber of Commerce of the United States, *Policy Declarations* (Washington, D.C., 1957).

device available to assist them in their task. The inter-state compact and interstate compact agencies can play a tremendous role in the states' reassumption of power. For there are no necessary limitations on the nature of the assignments interstate compact agencies may be given, nor any arbitrary restrictions on the fields into which they may enter. They may be endowed with all the powers states ordinarily give to local governmental units or entrust to agencies within their several bound-aries, including the power of eminent domain, the power to tax, and, if the states wish it so, the power to enforce their own orders.

Moreover, they can help the states tackle problems with the least drain on their financial resources. In every attempt by a state to reassert itself the crucial question of finances will arise. Even if it should become possible for the federal government to release some of its tax sources to the states, it is doubtful if many states, by themselves, could greatly add to the number of programs they are already carrying and still provide adequate service to their citizens. But together, in actions based on agreement through compact and through a com-mon interstate administrative mechanism, the states can greatly increase their effectiveness. For each problem which states attack jointly frees each state of much of the expense of adding an agency to its own administra-tive machinery and permits the use of its resources to greater advantage in other directions.

If compacts are to be more widely used in the future, the process of getting a compact through Congress should be greatly facilitated by Congress itself. Every compact must be submitted to Congress for approval, and Congress has no efficient procedure to follow. Not only have an increasing number of compacts been submitted since World War II, but this has been the very period when Congress' work in other areas has become increasingly complex, the sessions longer, and the tempers shorter. One result has been that bills granting consent to compacts have often been delayed without any opportunity to be heard. To remedy the situation, the National Association of Attorneys General has recommended to Congress a bill, which Senator Alan Bible submitted to the 85th Congress on March 10, 1958. That bill, S. 3428, or an equivalent measure, should be passed. Briefly, the bill provides an optional procedure by which copies of any compact may be transmitted to the President and the Congress automatically and their consent shall be deemed to have been granted if at the end of ninety days of continuous session thereafter Congress shall not have taken negative action. In Senator Bible's words, "more expeditious procedures, such as contemplated by this bill, appear highly desirable as an encouragement to states . . . to cooperate for more effective discharge of their services and activities on behalf of the people." [11]

Better financial support for existing compact agencies is also a great need. Because many agencies have done so well on such small appropriations from each state, the states have come to think that they do not need much larger ones. But inflation on the one hand and the discovery of new opportunities for service on the other have

[11] 104 *Congressional Record* 3307, March 10, 1958.

made many compact agency budgets inadequate. The chief effect of the limited budgets on which most compact agencies operate is of course understaffing. One of the results of understaffing has been the necessity of relying on lay committees or on state or federal officers for the performance of some or much of the work which would ordinarily be done by a staff. If in practice a commendable record has been made on the whole by such committees, it has meant all the same reliance on voluntary, unpaid work, with all the disadvantages that entails. Reliance either on committees or on state or federal officers for the performance of agency work means that that work is handled by individuals who have no direct responsibility for it—individuals to whom compact business is secondary to their regular, full-time work. The compact commissioners, meeting only periodically as they do, and in every case fully occupied in other directions as they are, must depend for the most part on committee action and recommendations. Without adequate staffs of their own, they become in a sense prisoners of their committees or of the officers, state or federal, who act for them.

To provide a larger financial base for the existing agencies and to make it possible for new compact agencies to operate from the beginning without a financial handicap will require a much broader and deeper knowledge and understanding of compacts and compact agencies than exists today. The agencies themselves will have to take the leadership in achieving such an understanding, but the press might assist them by devoting more space to their accomplishments.

Some Conclusions and Predictions

Finally, it would seem necessary to develop closer liaison between compact agencies and state legislatures. In the long run, compact agencies can go only as far as the legislatures allow. Freedom of movement can be secured only on the basis of understanding. In this matter, the legislatures themselves should take the initiative.

For years, the use of compacts was confined to situations in which "but one decision was required" and in which "continuing problems needing constant or frequent adjustment" did not arise.[12] The development of the compact agency and the demonstration of its utility in the last twenty years, however, has placed it in a dynamic and increasingly complex situation. As the states seek ways to exercise their own powers, they will undoubtedly utilize the compact more frequently and, as each compact agency proves its value in practice, the states will be reinforced in their decision to create new agencies. It is yet possible that compact agencies may become a widely accepted and familiar governmental form in the United States.

[12] Odum and Moore, *American Regionalism*, 206.

Bibliographical Note

There is a considerable literature on the subject of interstate compacts *qua* compacts. A good starting place is the Council of State Government's publication, *Interstate Compacts 1783–1956* (Chicago, 1956), which lists all the compacts ratified in the United States during those years, both by party states and chronologically. The four-page introduction and the chart and map on pages 5 and 6 are a great help too. For analytical treatment of compacts, the Frankfurter and Landis article referred to above (see Footnote #5, 9 *supra*) is a necessary beginning. Another early publication valuable as background and because of its effect in promoting the general use of compacts is Northcutt Ely, *Oil Conservation through Interstate Agreement* (Washington: Federal Oil Conservation Board, 1933). The National Resources Committee's 1935 report *Regional Factors in National Planning and Development* (Washington, D.C., 1935), chs. 6 and 7, should also be consulted, as should Jane Perry Clark's remarks in her *The Rise of a New Federalism* (New York, 1938), 71–80.

Bibliographical Note

The first really definitive and general treatment of compacts was made by Frederick L. Zimmermann and Mitchell Wendell in *The Interstate Compact Since 1925* (Chicago, 1951), which has been cited in the foregoing pages. It takes up where Frankfurter and Landis left off and brings the story down to 1950, covering the evolution and making of compacts, their legal aspects, the problems encountered in enforcing them and in federal participation, and it concludes with an admirable chapter on compacts and American federalism. Throughout it emphasizes recent developments in the use of compacts. Since both authors speak from long personal experience with the formulation of compacts (Mr. Zimmermann is Research Director of the New York Joint Legislative Committee on Interstate Cooperation and Professor of Political Science at Hunter College; Mr. Wendell is Professor of Political Science at American International College) their book is all the more valuable. Vincent V. Thursby's *Interstate Cooperation: A Study of the Interstate Compact* (Washington, D.C., 1953), the only other book devoted to compacts, is less revealing.

In addition, there are a great many articles and shorter treatments on virtually every aspect of the negotiation, ratification, approval, and interpretation of compacts. An early bibliography of leading articles is Clifford H. Stone (ed.), *Interstate Compacts: A Compilation of Articles from Various Sources* (Denver, 1946), a publication of the Colorado Water Conservation Board. A more recent bibliography was compiled by the Subcommittee on Intergovernmental Relations of the Committee on Government Operations of the U.S. House of Representatives. It appears in *Intergovernmental Relations in the United States. A Selected Bibliography* (Committee Print, 84th Congress, 2nd Session, November, 1956), 53–59.

Although a great deal has been written on compacts—on the way they are negotiated and drawn up, on the process by which the consent of Congress is secured, on the problems encountered in enforcing them, and on the development of judicial opinion concerning them—the experience of interstate compact agencies at work, the subject of this study, has been almost entirely neglected. Although as long ago as 1949, James W. Fesler voiced his concern that interstate cooperation by compact had been inadequately explored and concluded that "we need to know more about . . . the machinery and the dynamics" of compact agency operation,[1] virtually no attention has been paid to compact agencies as such. Their functions and procedures, their machinery and methods, and the success they have achieved in attaining the goals of their respective compacts—all these have been studied superficially, if at all.

Political scientists have by and large ignored the existence of compact agencies altogether, and very few studies in public administration make any mention of them, to say nothing of giving attention to their operational aspects. Nor have the operations of individual compact agencies been subjected to any orderly investigation. Emil J. Sady, in a recent report to The Brookings Insti-

[1] James W. Fesler, *Area and Administration* (University, Alabama, 1949), 149.

tution, noted that despite "their distinctive features and importance, interstate bodies have not been the subject of systematic critical study" and concluded that a great deal of research is necessary on "the special problems involved in [their] creation, organization, financing, public control, and use. . . ." [2]

Only a small beginning has been made in the direction indicated by Sady and that only with regard to a few compact agencies. The Port of New York Authority has been the subject of intensive study over the years. In 1942, Erwin W. Bard revised and enlarged his doctoral dissertation at Columbia University into a monograph on *The Port of New York Authority* (New York, 1942). It is mostly an historical treatment of the Port Authority as it developed during the first twenty years of its existence, but it contains some excellent insights into the operation and administration of the Authority. Ch. IX is perhaps the most valuable from this point of view. Then in 1948, Frederick L. Bird, Director of Municipal Research for Dun and Bradstreet, attempted under commission from the Authority to make "a comprehensive review" of its progress. The result was published under the title, *A Study of the Port of New York Authority* (New York, 1949). Although its orientation is chiefly in the direction of Authority financing, several chapters are devoted to the organizational and operational aspects of the Authority. A great many shorter and more specialized studies of various aspects of the Authority's work have also been made. The Authority's own publication, *A Selected Bibliogra-*

[2] Sady, *Research in Federal-State Relations*, 45.

phy 1921-1956 (New York, 1956) lists well over 1000 entries. Many of the items are speeches of members of the Authority or of its staff or are publications or reports of the Authority which may be had only on interlibrary loan from the library of the Authority, and many are of a technical nature. However, a score or more entries deal with the administration and management, the financing and the staffing, and the way in which the functions of the Authority are carried out in practice. Especially worthwhile are the perceptive address by Matthias E. Lukens, Assistant Director of the Authority, before the 1953 meeting of the American Political Science Association, "The Port of New York Authority: A Case Study of an Interstate Mechanism"; the article, "How Should Authorities Be Controlled," *GAR Reporter*, September–December, 1953, pp. 73–74 ff.; and the remarks of Victor Jones in his *The Future of Cities and Urban Redevelopment* (Chicago, 1953), 583–86. The latest, and one of the best, accounts is the address, "The Port of New York Authority—A Public Agency Created by Interstate Compact," delivered by Sidney Goldstein, General Counsel of the Authority, at the Symposium on Atomic Energy and State Governments, Dallas, April 17, 1958.

The Southern Regional Education Board has also received considerable attention. A bibliography of both the publications of the Board and articles about the Board is regularly appended to the Board's brochure, *The Southern Regional Education Program*, copies of which may be secured by writing the Southern Regional Education Board. The analysis of the Board given by

Bibliographical Note

Leonard D. White in his *The States and the Nation* (Baton Rouge, 1953), 85–90, is especially incisive; and a more detailed account may be found in Redding S. Sugg, Jr.'s article, "Regionalism in Higher Education," *Journal of Higher Education*, XXVII (February, 1956), 73–80. The Board has announced that a book-length report on its first decade of operation will appear in 1959.

The Interstate Oil Compact Commission has been subjected to examination off and on since its creation in 1935. Blakely M. Murphy's "The Administrative Mechanism of the Interstate Compact to Conserve Oil and Gas: the Interstate Oil Compact Commission," *Tulane Law Review*, XXII (March, 1948), 384–402, is an earlier study; and Richard H. Leach, "The Interstate Oil Compact: A Study in Success," *Oklahoma Law Review*, X (August, 1957), 274–88, is a more recent one. Erick W. Zimmermann gives brief attention to the Commission in his *Conservation in the Production of Petroleum: A Study in Industrial Control* (New Haven, 1957), 205–210, 226–27. And the three reports made by the Attorney General of the United States at the direction of Congress, described in the text (see *supra*, 53–54), are very good analyses of the Commission's operations.

W. E. Leuchtenburg, *Flood Control Politics* (Cambridge, 1953) provides information about the origins of the Connecticut River Valley Flood Control Commission but appears to over-stress the effects of a public power–private power struggle in the development of this agency. Reuel L. Olson, *The Colorado River Compact* (privately printed, 1926) supplies much of the background necessary for an understanding of the Upper

Colorado River Commission. Milton M. Kinsey, "The Bi-State Development Agency for the Missouri-Illinois Metropolitan District," *American Planning and Civic Annual* (1951), 53–58, describes the then brand-new Bi-State Development Agency. The Executive Secretary of the Northeastern Interstate Forest Fire Protection Commission, Arthur S. Hopkins, reported in some detail on the operations of his Commission to the 1954 meeting of the Society of American Foresters. A transcript of his remarks is carried in the *1954 Proceedings—Society of American Foresters Meeting*, pp. 167–168. The operations of four Southwestern interstate water apportionment agencies (the Rio Grande Compact Commission, the Pecos River Commission, the Canadian River Commission, and the Sabine River Compact Administration) are described by Richard H. Leach in "The Interstate Compact, Water and the Southwest: A Case Study in Compact Utility," *Southwestern Social Science Quarterly*, XXXVIII (December, 1957), 236–47. H. R. Stinson discusses "Western Interstate Water Compacts" in the *California Law Review*, 45 (December, 1957), 655–64.

But about the bulk of the compact agencies presently operating today, there is nothing at all of this nature to turn to. The interested student must not give up, however, because he will find that the lack of attention devoted to compact agencies in the literature of political science and public administration is not due to the lack of raw material from which to work. Of that there is a great deal; most of it is rather readily available, and free at that. The publications of the agencies themselves are treasure troves of material. Not every agency publishes an annual report, but the reports of the agencies which do should certainly be consulted. The annual reports of the Port of New York Authority, the Delaware River Port Authority, the Waterfront Commission of New York Harbor, the Ohio River Valley Water Sanitation Commission, and the New England Interstate Water Pollution Control Commission are all exceptionally well done and offer great reward to those who read them through. The three marine fisheries agencies and several of the water apportionment agencies also publish reports, but on the whole they are more inclined to be concerned with technical matters and thus are less interesting to the student of operation and administration. Copies of all these reports are available upon request from the various commissions concerned.

A good many compact agencies publish regular newsletters, for which it is an easy matter to get on the mailing list. A simple postcard request in most cases will do. The Southern Regional Education Board publishes *Regional Action* at fairly regular intervals; the Western Interstate Commission for Higher Education, *Higher Education in the West;* and the New England Board of Higher Education, *Higher Education in New England.* The Interstate Commission on the Potomac River Basin publishes an excellent monthly *News Letter,* as does the New England Interstate Water Pollution Control Commission, and the Interstate Oil Compact Commission's *Compact Comments,* also published monthly, is equally good.

Some of the agencies make a practice of publishing

occasional pieces descriptive of their operations and procedures and intentionally designed to explain the agency to the public. Some of these are very good. The Southern Regional Education Board's brochure, *The Southern Regional Educational Program*, the Western Interstate Commission for Higher Education's pamphlet, *From Idea to Reality: The Progress and Potentials of the Western Interstate Commission for Higher Education*, and the Interstate Sanitation Commission's report, *Cleaning Up the Doorway to America*, all currently in print, are especially noteworthy. And the brochure distributed by the Interstate Commission on the Potomac River Basin, *The Interstate Commission on the Potomac River Basin, Its Policy and Program* (1946), has by no means lost its pertinency. Usually if one is on the mailing list of a compact agency for one type of publication, all such occasional reports will be sent along automatically.

Although the present study has been concerned only with agencies established by interstate compact, the administration of compacts by other means, chiefly through associations of the officials of already constituted state agencies, should not be neglected. The Parole and Probation Compact Administrators' Association, the Juvenile Compact Administrators' Association, and the Mental Health Compact Administrators' Association hold annual meetings the reports and minutes of which constitute an important source. These usually appear only in mimeographed form but are reproduced in whole or in part in the annual report of the New York Joint Legislative Committee on Interstate Cooperation. In addition, the Parole and Probation Compact Administrators have a comprehensive manual which is important as a working tool but not generally available in libraries. The first edition of a similar manual for the Juvenile Compact Administrators is now in preparation. One should also see the *Handbook on Interstate Crime Control*, published in Chicago by the Council of State Governments.

The publications of the agencies themselves are not the only raw material available. More, for a few compact agencies at least, may be found in the annual reports of the Commissions on Interstate Cooperation (or their equivalents) which are sent to the legislatures of three or four of the states party to some of the more important compacts. The reports of the New York Joint Legislative Committee on Interstate Cooperation to the legislature of that state, and those of the Massachusetts Commission on Interstate Cooperation to the General Court of Massachusetts, regularly contain information about the compact agencies to which those states are parties; and the reports of the New Jersey, Kansas, and Pennsylvania Commissions often do. In some cases, Congressional hearings may be utilized, particularly if the object is to ascertain what the framers of a particular compact visualized as the role of the compact agency to be established. Since virtually all compacts are submitted to Congress for approval, this type of prospective analysis is available for almost all compact agencies.

At least worth looking at in terms of material related to the operation of compact agencies are: 1) The list of doctoral dissertations carried annually in the *American Political Science Review*, where quite often a likely looking title turns up, and interlibrary loan or microfilm makes the manuscript itself fairly easy to obtain; 2) the technical literature in each subject-matter area in which compact agencies are employed—water supply, stream pollution, conservation, recreation, port operation, etc. Journals of political science and public administration have no monopoly on descriptions and analyses of compact agencies; 3) newspapers—although the daily press does not often pay attention to compact agencies, local papers are apt to give some coverage to the meetings of compact commissions held in the cities of their region, and sometimes a good deal of information is transmitted, especially when interviews with commission and staff members are reported; 4) the regular publications of the many university bureaus of public administration or government research, which occasionally venture into the field of compact agency operation; and 5) the literature in the general area of federal-state relations, which has increased tremendously since the Kestnbaum Commission report was made. Although compacts lie a little outside the focus of most such literature, enough about them is present to warrant considerable riffling of pages.

It should also be noted that the current activities of interstate compact agencies are reported regularly, if briefly, in the pages of the magazine called *State Government*, the quarterly publication of the Council of State Governments, and that the activities of some agencies are described somewhat more at length in the biannual *Book of the States*. Quite often, also, *State Government* carries special articles devoted to specific compacts and compact agencies, as it has from time to time on the Ohio River Valley Water Sanitation Commission and the Southern Regional Education Board. *State Government*, in fact, is the only publication which gives regular coverage to compact agencies and their activities.

All told, however, the amount of material either directly about or at least partially concerned with compact agencies is comparatively small. About some agencies—the Breaks Interstate Park Commission, the Tennessee-Missouri Bridge Commission, the Yellowstone River Compact Commission, for example—the most diligent searching produces nothing at all of any value; and it takes heavy digging to find much more of any worth about a number of other agencies. About a handful of compact agencies, a good deal is known; about the rest, virtually nothing. Taken as a whole, compact agency operation is still largely unexplored territory. Because of the growing importance of compact agencies as administrative bodies, it is logical to expect that the amount of research devoted to their methods and procedures will be sharply increased in the immediate future.

Already a number of studies are reported under way. The Southwestern Legal Foundation is engaged in research on "the attributes, capabilities and limitations of the interstate compact as a mechanism of state legal control" as a part of a study it is doing for the Southern Governors Conference on the methods the Southern states might use to regulate the development of nuclear energy. Professor Roscoe Martin of Syracuse University is engaged in a study of the feasibility of an interstate compact agency as the administrative arm of an interstate river development program. The focus of that study too will be on the effectiveness of compact agency operation, based on close study of a number of existing compact agencies. Professor Gilbert White of the University of Chicago and Norman A. Stoll, a Portland, Oregon, lawyer, are also studying various aspects of water resources development and the possible utility of compact agencies in that connection.

Index

Alley, Lawrence R., 126
American Fisheries Society, 174
American Legislators' Association, 11
American Political Science Review, as source on compact administration, 239f.
Anderson, Robert C., 126
Arkansas River Compact, sets membership qualifications, 65, 75; withholds enforcement power, 96
Arkansas River Compact Administration, classified, 19; relies on state and Federal agencies for staff, 117f.
Articles of Confederation, provision for interstate agreements (Article VI), 4
Assembly of the States, 23
Association of Attorney-Generals, 174
Atlantic States Marine Fisheries Commission, classified, 19; required to report to Congress, 54f.; divided into Sections, 83, 168f.; must share powers with intra-state agencies, 89; restricted in research, 89, 90, 98, 102; staff size, 121; responsibilities of Secretary-Treasurer, 128, 130; case study of, 157, 167–76; designed to conserve fisheries, 167f.; membership, 168; Sections of, described, 168f.; use, of advisory groups, 169f.; of special committees, 170; concern with research and recommendation, 170f.; use of other agencies for research, 171; striped bass project, 171f.; reasons for abstaining from research, 172; services to party states, 172–74; represents fishery interests, 174; budget, 174f.; authorized to establish

243

Western Interstate Commission on Higher Education, classified, 20; aided by U. S. Public Health Service, 59f.; conceives itself as "catalyst," 90, 92, 98, 102; relies on advisory committees, 104; staff size, 122; personnel policy, 122f.; has standing personnel committee, 124, 130, 131, 132, 136, 202

Wigmore, John H., 8

Wilson, F. C., article cited, 10n.

Wolverton, Charles A., quoted, 197

Yellowstone River Compact, specifies cooperation of Federal officials, 58; provision for appointment of U. S. member disapproved, 71

Yellowstone River Compact Commission, classified, 19; contracts with U. S. Geological Survey, 59; purpose of meetings, 100f.; contracts for engineering and clerical services, 118; chairman a U. S. G. S. engineer, 119; contracts for operation of gaging stations, 120

Young, Edgar B., quoted, 148

Zimmermann, Frederick L., i; articles cited, 168n. *See also* Wendell, Mitchell L. and Frederick L. Zimmermann

Zimmermann, Frederick L., and Mitchell Wendell, quoted, 14, 222